PRESSING
THE RIGHT
BUTTONS

PRESSING THE RIGHT BUTTONS

people skills for
business success

ALLISON MOONEY

RANDOM HOUSE
NEW ZEALAND

A catalogue record for this book is available from the National Library of New Zealand

A RANDOM HOUSE BOOK
published by
Random House New Zealand
18 Poland Road, Glenfield, Auckland, New Zealand
www.randomhouse.co.nz

Random House International
Random House
20 Vauxhall Bridge Road
London, SW1V 2SA
United Kingdom

Random House Australia (Pty) Ltd
20 Alfred Street, Milsons Point, Sydney,
New South Wales 2061, Australia

Random House South Africa Pty Ltd
Isle of Houghton
Corner Boundary Road and Carse O'Gowrie
Houghton 2198, South Africa

Random House Publishers India Private Ltd
301 World Trade Tower, Hotel Intercontinental Grand Complex,
Barakhamba Lane, New Delhi 110 001, India

First published 2007. Reprinted 2008 (twice)

© 2007 Allison Mooney

The moral rights of the author have been asserted

ISBN 978 1 86941 903 5

Text design: Kate Greenaway
Cover design: Katy Yiakmis
Printed by Griffin

Contents

Introduction

Fog-bound at the airport — personality types in action

Imagine a cold winter's day at the airport, the fog slowly rolling in. In one of the many frequent-flyer lounges, an announcement over the PA brings everyone to a standstill. 'Ladies and gentlemen, the airport is now closed due to fog, and all aircraft are grounded. We apologise for any inconvenience caused. A further announcement will be made as soon we get an update on weather conditions.'

This was a regular occurrence in my role as a manager of one of these frequent-flyer lounges. No two days were ever the same, and we always had passengers who added extra flavour and colour.

It's easy to visualise the pandemonium that follows one such announcement — and how different people react to it. Let's go there for a moment . . .

The most noticeable person is an attractive, very flamboyant lady, her clothes screaming 'look at me, look at me!'. It's an outfit you couldn't help but notice, completed by dangly earrings, matching necklace, perfectly applied make-up and eye-catching matching shoes. She limps as she walks because those shoes don't necessarily fit, but she is such a package that it is obvious she is not about to complain about them. No shoe is too small when fashion is involved!

As she reaches down to her handbag to answer her cellphone, you can't help notice the tattoo, positioned in a conspicuous place: a happy little logo, nothing dark or devious, that would bring a smile to anyone's face. It seems to be there solely as a conversation starter.

Her handbag is open, spilling with copious amounts of stuff — things like plasters, paper clips, insulation tape, a bountiful selection of pens, a rotten apple core (mouldy), a knife and a couple of toothbrushes, phone numbers written on serviettes and scraps of paper, belonging to long-lost friends that she has yet to ring. Her wallet is another story, bulging with receipts, old concert tickets, speeding tickets yet to be paid. The handbag describes her to a T — open — but only because it's so over-full that it can't close.

Her well-manicured hands, decked out with jewellery that demands compliments, move continuously as she speaks. In fact, even if you taped up her mouth, you could still understand her message through all the gesturing and animation.

She is a warm, friendly soul, smiling at everyone, and loud with it. Her voice has lots of inflection and variety of pitch, to the point of nearly singing. You can hear her above everyone else. But what is most notable about her is her ability to initiate contact with people. She is fascinating to observe, giving a free lesson in the art of networking, speaking with ease despite all the commotion, whether people are listening or not. Despite the setback, it's obvious that she's in top form: not the least bit concerned who is approving or disapproving, nor about her next plan, but interested in the new 'friends' she might meet because of the disruption.

As an airline staff member passes her, she suggests he might like to open the bar — even though it's only 7 a.m. Obligingly, he puts on the light, fills the jugs with iced water and without words opens his arms to indicate 'go for it'.

Our 'standout' takes her cue, rising quickly and abandoning her handbag on the seat. She quickly joins the others who are heading in the same direction, carrying a handful of business cards, ready to form new relationships. It seems a natural course of action to initiate contact with all those who have the same idea. Her mouth never stops moving from the moment she is in earshot of anyone prepared to listen.

Another group of people also catches the eye, a mixture of men and women who have a strong, commanding presence. They congregate at the service desk, demanding immediate attention, in unison or over each other, their fists are hitting the counter, their eyes moving quickly and necks turning red. Flashing their gold elite member cards, they are insisting they get priority attention and be moved to the front of the queue, expecting immediate recognition and favours. Their authoritative voices turn heads. Power and prestige radiate from them.

The airline staff member being confronted looks grateful for the protection the desk provides as she tries desperately to recall the last customer service conflict resolution course she has been on. You can see her muttering under her breath words like 'nodding', 'listening,' 'eye contact', 'show empathy' and 'engagement' as they all talk over each other, not even aware of her lips moving. They point their index fingers right at her. Their body language speaking louder than their words: pursed lips, puffing chest, pacing back and forth, at the same time speaking in a tone that would send most people scurrying for the nearest exit.

'When is the fog going to lift?' (As if the poor staff member knows!)

'I have a meeting to take, a very important meeting!'

'What are you going to do for us?'

'I haven't time to sit around here!'

'How long does it take to drive to . . . ?'

'Doesn't this card stand for anything?'

This group, while making unreasonable demands of the poor airline staff member, are also talking into their phones, doing business. Very rarely are the words 'please' or 'thank you' mentioned. Comments like 'Incompetence!', 'I don't have the luxury of spare time', 'I'm stuck at the airport', 'I am too busy to have this happen!' and 'I am interested to see what the airline is going to do about this mess' convey a sense of importance to those surrounding them.

It's interesting to see that these types, when they shoot from the mouth and give orders, seem to get what they want — probably because those who they are talking at want to get rid of them as quickly as possible!

Moving from the high-tension situation at the service desk — which looks more like a stock exchange with tickets, voices and arms jostling for position — to the other end of the lounge, a more unobtrusive group is forming. These people are searching for a quiet area, a mobile-free zone. They are definitely not sitting together, but moving as far away from the noise as they can possibly get.

These are impeccably dressed types, with high-tech accessories. The women look as if they are straight out of *Vogue* magazine, with straight bob haircuts and dark, well-made suits. The men have hair so manicured it looks as if it is kept together with hairspray and starch. They look ready to step out on the Armani catwalk. Nothing is out of place for these very controlled, formal, well-mannered types. As they get up out of their chairs, they dust their clothes and adjust them, from ties and cufflinks to socks, checking to make sure everything is presentable.

Their laptops are open on the tables, and they are intent on checking their diaries, palmtops, tablets, voicemail etc. Everything they carry is state of the art. Displayed on the screens of their PCs are two lists, one highlighted in red and one in black: Plan A and Plan B.

It's not the words that are said, but the quiet muttering under their breath, the tsking, the sighing, the shaking their heads in exasperation, that shows what they might be feeling. Their purposeful body language is easier to read than what they have to say. It is evident that they are not pleased about this interruption to their day.

When an airline staff member approaches one of them, the conversation as she hands him his ticket is intriguing to say the least. This passenger asks so many questions. Every time the airline employee attempts to move away, he says, 'Oh, by the way . . .' It's as if he is dumping all the data that is on his mind onto her, as he is forced to rearrange his schedule. He adopts a more calculating face, showing signs of concern, as he sits back down and revisits his thoughts, processing them then updating his mind.

This is in direct contrast to the group over at the bar, who seem to have abandoned any thought about getting to the next destination. They're sharing stories about the last time this happened to them and all that went on, embroidering the conversation with anecdotes about life's little disasters. You can see these people are enjoying themselves as they explode into great belly laughs, encouraging others to join them by searching for someone giving them eye contact. Some have arms around each other's shoulders, giving reassuring hugs, within moments of making a connection. They're obviously there to have fun and aren't the slightest bit interested in leaving such a fascinating group of people, or the lovely place in which they have to wait it out. The impeccably dressed formal types are watching in disbelief.

One more group is also forming. It is their relaxed manner that gives them away. Newspapers sprawled out in front of them on the coffee tables, they are observing all that is going on. Most are sitting stretched out with their hands behind their heads, and those standing are leaning against a pole or wall if possible. They are happy to wait until given the next instruction by those in the know, content to go along with what's happening and not at all fazed.

Their clothing looks uncomplicated — not messy, but perhaps more casual than others. Open-neck shirts, sweatshirts and trackpants are preferred, and the trainers on their feet give them away. There seem to be more men with beards than in the other groups, but it's their hair that distinguishes them most. It has no defined style, or as much effort put in compared with the other groups. In fact, effort seems to be something they shy away from. They are dressed for comfort not for style. A t-shirt and jeans will take them anywhere.

These are very pleasant people, who listen well and enjoy the company of others — 'go with the flow' types who avoid conflict at all costs.

This is a situation that would occur at airports all over the world on any given bad-weather day. You may have experienced it yourself.

As we can see from the scenario above, different people see and hear the same words and messages, but respond in different ways. They process the information differently. So how on earth can we relate to others who view their world completely differently?

Unfortunately, I was six years into my career in the airline industry before I discovered a powerful, easy-to-use tool which gave me insight into people's behaviours and responses, and taught me how to read them, and more importantly how to effectively relate to them. This tool, when used in the right context, enabled me to have a totally different response from the usual reactions when things didn't go right. I could use it not only when things went wrong, but to motivate others the way they would like to be motivated. I started to love coming to work every day — and even enjoy disruptions!

Once I discovered this simple key, and started using it, there was a dramatic shift in my own performance, and an improvement in my relationships with my staff, passengers and, for that matter, those close to me at home! I could access this potent, effective tool anytime.

So what is this key that meant I could send those people in that lounge away feeling significantly valued and happy to return, even though they weren't able to leave the airport on time? Being able to 'speed read' people: observing the behaviours and characteristics of others, identifying their primary traits so I could effectively relate to them in the way they wanted to be related to, and knowing what to look for in order to speak the language they understood.

The hot issues in the business marketplace today are staff retention, skill shortages, a tight labour market and employment tribunal problems. These are impacting enormously on the bottom line and are of huge concern to business owners.

The feedback I get from company leaders is that one of the main reasons people get restless and want to leave their jobs is because of difficulties they have with a fellow colleague: we call them 'personality clashes'. Leaders also often suffer from an inability to motivate, move and inspire people. The incredible investment that goes in to training a new recruit, only to have them leave because of their frustration at being undervalued, costs organisations millions of dollars every year, when the application of a few basic 'people skills' would have kept them there.

This is the essence of what this book is about: people skills that will bring success to any business. It's about understanding how people are wired, and giving them what they need in keeping with their personality. Let's get a handle on what that really means . . .

 The complexity of people

People can be complicated, can't they? But when we know something about our personalities, things become a lot more simple.

Whatever situation you may be in, understanding what motivates others and what their focus is means you can communicate more effectively, appreciate and respect the differences in others and generally improve business and personal relationships. This will dramatically change the way you see yourself and others. It can enhance and improve just about every aspect of your life.

The first question that is usually asked about personality is whether it is carried in our genes (nature) or developed over time (nurture). This debate has been around for the longest time.

I believe that, regardless of our upbringing or circumstances, we are born with a temperament: raw material unique to us. Of course, over time it gets moulded and shaped by events and influences as we go through life, but the 'personality' or 'type' we were born with is with us forever. Some would say that the temperament we are born with is expressed through our personality, in the form of behaviours, characteristics and traits.

Think of yourself as a block of wood, with all the beauty of its natural grain and form. As your life moves forward, the grain remains the same, but the shape and definition changes as outside elements affect the piece of wood. If you were a piece of driftwood, storms, wind, gales, sun and the force of the tide would keep battering your shape and honing it into something unique, yet its original grain would be preserved. These elements are factors such as childhood and adult experiences, culture, belief systems and birth order, which add to the personality that you have been given.

While each person is wired differently, there are many similarities that allow us to be classified into general descriptions. Now this is where some people react, saying 'I don't want to be categorised'. Well, neither do I, and it's not my intention. I just want to offer a framework to help us understand others more effectively.

Now before any macho guys react to the word 'emotional', what I mean is that we all have an invisible tank inside us that needs filling. Different personalities seek to have it filled in certain ways. We respond and make decisions because of this need.

Identifying someone's personality is just the initial framework. What matters is giving them what they need, which I believe is critical to getting it right with people. We miss the target so often when we direct what *we* need at those we are relating to. If you want to get along with others successfully, doesn't it make sense to give them what lights them up?

This is not a new science. The four personality groupings were first established by Hippocrates some 2400 years ago. (I am sure that those of a certain personality will love reading the following, and some will want to skip over this!) For the Greeks, recognising and understanding behavioural styles was an integral part of their wellbeing. They believed that the body contained four fundamental liquids, called humours. When one of these humours became dominant over the others, it was thought to impact on the person's mood and general approach.

The four humours — blood, yellow bile, phlegm and black bile — were each believed to be responsible for a different type of behaviour. An excess of blood made a person Sanguine, which related to high energy and optimism. Yellow bile resulted in a Choleric nature, connected to control and anger, while phlegm naturally produced a Phlegmatic outlook — peaceful, passive and stolid. Black bile was associated with Melancholia, but also depth of intelligence.

Hippocrates, the father of medicine, was the first to set down these theories in a methodical and systematic way, which was embraced and used until the Middle Ages. Of course, we have since discovered this methodology has no basis in human biology, but what the Greeks achieved was the first method of describing man's behaviour. So successful was their approach that some of the terms are used even today: humour (in the sense of mood), sanguine, phlegmatic and melancholic.

Thankfully, current personality testing does not rely on measuring the amount of black bile in a person, but many of the concepts behind modern testing can be traced back to Hippocrates' theories. Many modern hypotheses of personal behaviour are rooted in the idea of these four individual types. The Swiss psychologist Carl Jung was one who believed that people instinctively respond and understand people through the operation of these four variables.

Below is a chart showing some of the many different personality-type systems used today. All are based on Hippocrates' work, but with different names.

PERSONALITY TYPES COMPARISON CHART

HIPPOCRATES	Sanguine	Choleric	Melancholy	Phlegmatic
PERSONALITY PLUS US (Florence Littauer)	Popular	Powerful	Perfect	Peaceful
PERSONALITY PLUS NZ (Allison Mooney)	Playful	Powerful	Precise	Peaceful
LARRY CRABB	Emotional Expressive	Volitional Dominant	Rational Analytical	Personal Solid
SMALLEY & TRENT	Otter	Lion	Beaver	Golden Retriever
DISC SYSTEM	Influencing/ interacting	Dominance	Cautious/ compliance	Steadiness
ALESSANDRA & CATHCART	Socialiser	Director	Thinker	Relator

MERRILL-REID SOCIAL STYLES	Expressive	Driving	Analytical	Amiable
	Peacock	Eagle	Owl	Dove
RAINBOW CONNECTION	Blue	Red	Green	Yellow
TETRAPLAN	Fire	Earth	Wind	Water
COLOUR CODE	Yellow	Red	Blue	White
TRUE COLOURS	Orange	Gold	Green	Blue

If you read around this subject matter, you will find even more models. All of them, of course, are generalisations. No one person would fit perfectly into any one category because of the other contributing factors mentioned before. Most often people have a smidgen of other traits and that is what makes them uniquely them.

The model I use is based on the work of Florence and Marita (daughter of Florence and the late Fred) Littauer . I respect their work immensely, having trained with them as an Advanced Personality Trainer. I have altered their descriptions of the four types slightly to better fit with our local culture. Instead of using Perfect, I think Precise rings more true for us 'down under'. And instead of Popular, I have found Playful describes these types better for me. Powerful and Peaceful still fit well, however!

What I love about this tool is that it offers something more than just personality identification. It's based around meeting people's emotional needs. Using the above framework we can move forward to being better relationship builders. By the time you have finished reading this book, you will have a sound understanding of the four critical key factors of influence, and be able to quickly identify one in particular that speaks loudest about you. Celebrate that, and also learn how to readily distinguish the influences of others so you can better relate to them. Remember, no one personality type is better than the others . . . they are just different!

2 Why understanding personality is important at work

Every day the roads are filled with different people, heading in different directions with different goals in mind. Most of us drive along smoothly with few mishaps because we understand and obey some common laws. We stop at stop signs and red lights. We proceed on green lights. We drive within the speed limit.

However, in our relationships, both in the workplace and at home, we seem to have a few more bumps. We wish we could straighten out all those other people — those very same people who want to straighten us out!

Understanding the effects of personality is nothing short of amazing when it comes to navigating your own life and allowing others to navigate theirs. It is to communication and business relationships what traffic laws and road maps are to driving! Understanding the effects of personality provide guidelines and directions which show us how to function individually and together as we ride the road of life and attempt to live together in a harmonious and orderly manner, respecting our differences.

In business, people skills are imperative if we are to survive. Too often we invest more in technology than we do in our people. We can never, *never* overlook how important people are. The human spirit has an innate desire to connect. (As I wrote this book I experienced this to a great degree, as I was locked away from those who mean so much to me. There were times when I wanted to bail out because the isolation was almost overwhelming!)

Because we spend so many hours at our workplace, it's vital that we find ways of making this time more meaningful. As business owners, managers, colleagues or customers, we need to know how to do this. Couldn't we all benefit from knowing how to make every encounter more valuable and worthwhile?

If we took the time to get out of our own shoes and into the shoes of the people we are relating to, we would find our workplaces would run with less friction. Productivity and respect would increase and we would all find significance and value in what we do. Everyone would win!

Understanding this powerful tool can ignite your passion for people, as you learn to look at them through a different lens: theirs! You will be more effective in meetings and negotiations, and keep your staff both motivated and loyal. This is the key to unlocking those doors you may have previously struggled to open.

A question I ask people who attend my seminars is, 'How many of you have ever resigned from a job because of difficulties with someone you work with, or someone you have to have contact with for work?' It is at least one third of the group every time.

Now think about spending 40-plus hours a week in an environment like that. Who wants to be where someone is constantly giving them grief? What level of efficiency and productivity can there be with all the anxiety and stress of trying to relate to someone who doesn't even notice you, can't be bothered, or doesn't respect your contribution? It spells stress, burnout, blowout, then walk out!

Working in any organisation can be tough, demanding and frustrating at times. We often have to handle pressure from all sides. Sometimes our performance is dependent on the contributions of other people. We have to be kind to unkind people. We have to smile when all we want to do is finish our tasks and go home. When one thing goes wrong, everything seems to go wrong.

Yes, our positions often require technical skills, such as operating a computer, using an array of different equipment and learning processes, and keeping up with technology. However, our jobs also require 'people skills': communicating with others, working together to provide the best possible outcome, providing service, negotiating, handling several people at once, dealing with interruptions, handling crises, calming unhappy clients and much, much more.

We may offer similar products or services, but at the end of the day it is our people who will make or break our business.

I am confident that your staff and colleagues will stay loyal and be more committed to you if you make an effort to try to understand their uniqueness, listen through their ears and see the world through their eyes.

In conversations with business owners, managers and team leaders, I find their greatest challenge is the conflicts that arise from managing people. So much whining and whinging goes on, even by so-called leaders, with their direct reports, but they are oblivious to the fact that they are creating a toxic culture through their words. They then wake up one day to the realisation that they are working in a negative environment — ignorant of the fact that they were partly responsible for creating it. Their organisations then have to cough up huge amounts of money for training and development to challenge their thinking, perceptions and behaviours.

If only we could stop and look at how brilliant we all are, and how together we can do a whole lot more, drawing on each other's strengths.

There is nothing more exciting than seeing a leadership team sit around a table acknowledging each other's strengths, then strategically slotting them into the best possible roles to complete a task. When we focus on each other's strengths, our weaknesses tend to fade. They aren't so much of an issue any more, as everyone is energised by doing what they love doing.

The teams that I see working well are those that have at least one of each personality bringing their own style and flavour to the table. Conversely, a team that is top-heavy with one type can either cause insurrection, fighting, dissension in the ranks, loss of motivation — the list goes on — and it's not long before team members will start looking for another job! Great teams focus on each other's abilities and move forward respecting each other's strengths. This is a very powerful way to grow the business and the people.

3 How this tool has worked for me personally

This book would have no impact or power if I couldn't say how it has worked for me personally. I can't stress enough how getting to grips with the different personalities and how to relate to them has been critical in my personal development.

Of course, understanding personalities is not just a great tool to use in the workplace as a key to business growth and staff retention; it is equally powerful at home. Appreciating how differences can work together in a team, in an organisation, or in a marriage, we then know what to look for and how to communicate best with those we are relating to. I am confident that my marriage would not have the strength it has today had I not learned that we are each wired a certain way, and that different people need to communicate differently.

I can't believe how long it took me to find this precious tool. It was there all along, but as they say, we often don't change until the pain of not changing becomes too great.

I was well into my late 30s–early 40s before I started looking for and finding tools that would assist me on this road we call 'life'. Can you imagine what it felt like for me when an extraordinary couple, Florence and (the late) Fred Littauer visited New Zealand from the United States to speak on the subject of personalities? I sat in the audience transfixed, and devoured every word.

They came at a time when I was so ready. Forty is an interesting time in one's life — I believe it is a defining time. My children had grown up and I was looking at the next phase of my life. At this conference, I was like a dry sponge, soaking up every word they said.

After the seminar I made a bee-line towards the book table, and I arrived home with eleven books. For the next few weeks I read, re-read and consumed every word in these books.

It was uncanny. It was as if the Littauers had peeped into our lounge after a day's work and painted the picture I was living out. They seemed to describe the way I saw my world differently from how my husband saw it.

Just bringing home those books and my husband's response to them showed it. I am more into 'against all odds' books and motivational stories; he prefers history. My husband's idea of a pleasant, enjoyable night is no interruptions, no phone calls, a comfortable chair, the TV remote in his hand and a good night's telly: if possible the news first, then history or nature programmes, and of course the sports. He loves sport to bits. He's been known to watch games, video-record them, then watch them again! (Is that just a Kiwi bloke thing?) He constantly wars within himself over whether we should subscribe to Sky. Not because of the cost but because he knows himself well enough that he knows he would get hooked, and never turn the telly off again!

You could think that he was a little lazy. Don't get me wrong, he is far from that. He gets all his tasks done. He loves projects — he has a list of them, some completed and some not — and could tell you immediately what he has pending. He's very structured, and always completes everything that needs completing before the 6 o'clock news.

What I have discovered about him is that rest and relaxation are his rewards for a hard day's work. I didn't understand this until I learned about the different personalities. There are certain types just like him who are in their element living like this.

I couldn't be further from that, however. My reward for a hard day's work is catching up with friends, being around activity, trying new things and loving interruptions. The telly is the last thing I look forward to! I also don't mind a bit of clutter around. I can relax with the newspaper or magazines left on the table, and my shoes left in the lounge, whereas my husband can be a little edgy when things aren't put back in their proper place.

Now, isn't that interesting: two people attracted to each other who are so opposite in so many areas. On the outside, our marriage would seem set up for failure.

Fred and Florence Littauer were able to give me some insight into what I thought was a mystery. I applied their techniques and now, 17 years later, I find myself standing up in conferences, travelling to distant shores, and capturing people's interest by talking about this remarkable subject that seems to be the missing link in the incredible people puzzle.

Those 17 years have taken me on a ride that has stretched me, and unravelled and challenged my thinking and perceptions. I still enjoy the ports of call to which my journey takes me, with the same husband I have just written about.

That seems to be something of a rarity these days. I often have women come to me and say, 'Allison, my husband and I are so, so different. The only thing we have in common is that we got married on the same day!' This seems to give some people licence to leave their marriage — just because they are different. Could I suggest that after so much effort has been put into one's marriage, this doesn't have to be? And besides, from what I've heard, second time around only brings new and different challenges.

My husband and I also have two children. It always baffled me how they could be so different even though they had been raised under the same roof, with the same belief system and culture and similar childhood experiences.

Even early in the lives of my two prized and precious daughters I could easily see how different they were in the way they view their world. One has natural leadership tendencies. Growing up, she could organise all the kids in the neighbourhood. She was comfortable about challenging anyone who stepped out of line. A quick thinker, she loved being with people and being involved in lots of activities.

The other daughter had one special friend, would play for hours just with this one special person, and would avoid conflict at any price. She would most often give in to the 'take charge' sibling. One loved to be initiating the game, the other was happier to go along with what was being dished out. No one of those two was better: they were just different.

They are both adults now, and it is fascinating to see them being attracted to people who are opposite in traits to themselves. It seems we are most often naturally attracted to our opposite, craving the strengths they have for ourselves. Sadly, before marriage we are fascinated by these differences, but after marriage we can be frustrated by them! That happens when those attractive strengths are pushed out too far and then we view them negatively.

Our work life commands and demands a lot of our time. We need to feel happy in it. We need to feel we add to the big picture.

One of the challenges we face in these modern times is the way we pour ourselves into work and find our value in the *doing* part of who we are, instead of firstly *being*. In social situations, this is endorsed nearly every day: 'Hello, my name is . . .' And what comes next? 'And what do you do?'

Doing is not all wrong — for some people, this is their primary instinctive need and drive. But what about those poor souls for whom this isn't their motivation? I have come across many people struggling with this, plagued by questions like, 'Who am I really?', 'What is my significance?', 'How come I can't relate to certain people?', 'If I am not climbing the corporate ladder, does my life count?', 'What is success?' and so on. If we don't look and find answers to these questions, we will continue this way even into retirement, often missing out on truly living.

In order to find meaning, first we look at those needs we are trying to satisfy throughout our life, those urges that we spend a lot of time seeking to fulfil:

- to tap into the innovative part of us that imparts all of life (our creativity)
- to know and express our talents

- to feel that our lives matter, and that we will leave behind some kind of legacy.

In essence, living a good life means knowing our significance, having a place where we can express our strengths, and doing the right work: with purpose.

When we're not doing that, we become restless — and restlessness grows like a cancer. It can choke the life out of us, in the form of workaholism, divorce, having affairs, toxic relationships, throwing in the towel and quitting our jobs. I see far too many people like this out there: working in jobs they hate, often because they are operating out of their weaknesses, rather than expressing their strengths.

To me, finding out who I am, and being able to express my gifts and talents, has been a most beneficial and fulfilling experience. It's defined my authenticity, and given me a sharper focus on how to use the strengths which each of us has. And along the way, my relationships have run more smoothly as well.

The intention of this book is to help you, too, discover this for yourself — not only finding out about yourself, but also how you can get along better with others.

Now before a certain type mutters under their breath, 'I don't care if I don't get along with others, I just want to get the job done', please be patient and keep reading. I promise that if you apply these principles you will experience less stress (which, if you ask any doctor, is a killer). Using this simple tool will lead to greater success and satisfaction at work, and a greater feeling of fulfillment in your life in general. So, let's find out how . . .

4 The real you

This above all: to thine own self be true — SHAKESPEARE
We first must know ourselves, before we can understand or help others.
— FLORENCE LITTAUER

If you don't know your own strengths and capabilities, it's natural that you will be constantly trying to be what others expect you to be, and be run ragged trying to satisfy everyone else's whims. Too often we go around trying to be what we weren't designed to be, therefore getting frustrated with ourselves and others. It's like trying to lace your shoe with your 'other' hand — it takes heaps more energy. By knowing ourselves, we can be more confident as we operate out of our natural talents and personality, able to influence and achieve to a higher degree.

The mini profile on the next page will give you a quick overview of your basic personality, and help you to identify your primary and secondary quadrants. This exercise identifies your strengths. My preference is to work with these. In business, if we constantly focus on our team's strengths, rather than bemoaning their weaknesses, productivity will be higher and the general environment much better.

Instructions

Circle all the words and statements that you feel best describe you.

'Come on, it will be OK!'

'Let's not waste any more time and get moving!'

Enthusiastic	Friendly	Ambitious	Goal-driven
Outgoing	Loves variety	Decisive	Commands
Innovative	Imaginative	Enjoys challenges	Independent
Energetic	Playful	Quick	Visionary
Motivator	Positive	Single-minded	Productive
Social	Bubbly	Bold	Doer
Takes chances	Funloving	Likes to lead	Daring
Forgiving	Loves gatherings	Achievement-driven	Opinionated
Expressive	Open	Adventurous	Competitive
Enjoys new things	Animated	Decision-maker	Change agent
Talker	Promoter	Action oriented	Restless
Loyal	Balanced	High ideals	Well mannered
Patient	Dependable	Tidy	Persistent
Non-demanding	Understanding	Cool	Detailed
Level-headed	Mediator	Reserved	Calculating
Calming	Nurturing	Predictable	Loves the arts
Likes routine	Dry humour	Practical	Thorough
Dislikes change	Tolerant	Intentional	Critical thinker
Enjoyable	Good listener	Factual	On time
Accepting	Easy-going	Evaluates	Ordered
Steady	Willing	Cautious	Proper
Approachable	Relaxed	Particular	Musical

'Don't worry, be happy'

'A place for everything, and everything in its place!'

After you have completed circling the descriptive words that pertain to you:

1. Draw a line down the page after the 2nd column.
2. Draw a line across the page under TALKER and above LOYAL.

There are now four quadrants.

Add up all the words circled in each quadrant, then double each of these numbers. You should now have four totals.

The top left quadrant we'll call *Playful*, top right we'll call *Powerful*, bottom Left we'll call *Peaceful*, and bottom right we'll call *Precise*: the four P's.

Playful	*Powerful*
Peaceful	*Precise*

The highest score is your dominant personality type. If you have two scores the same, you are a blend of these two types. If you have an obvious high score in only one quadrant, you are probably strong in that particular type.

If you have three equal scores, the middle quadrant is likely to be your dominant type personality.

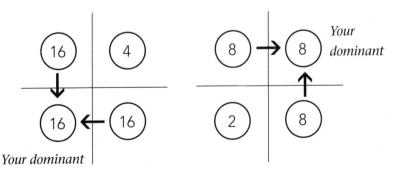

If you are pretty much the same in all four, you are probably a Peaceful type, as they can work best in and bend to any quadrant.

Learned combinations

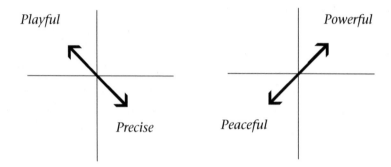

If you have come up with either Playful/Precise in combination or Peaceful/Powerful in combination, I believe these are not natural combinations, but it means you have chosen to exercise some traits that are learned. This can easily happen if you have been raised by someone who is strong in one of those quadrants, as opposed to revealing your 'natural' personality.

The Playful type is outgoing, while Precise is more self-contained and private. Peacefuls are non-confrontational, want harmony and would rather process things with no time pressure, while Powerfuls love a challenge and want to get things done *now*! Can you see the tension in these combinations? I don't believe we are born with these tensions; they get picked up or developed over time and through different circumstances.

If you have come up with these combinations, don't concern yourself. I promise you, you don't need therapy, but perhaps a little guidance to help you recognise your primary personality. It may be time to reflect on how you have been influenced.

As well as parental influences, we can also end up with odd combinations because our work requires us to do certain tasks that force us to develop strengths in other quadrants. When I was managing, I found I had to flex a lot into the Powerful quadrant. Getting aircraft off on time was the number one priority of each shift, otherwise the airline would have to pay huge amounts of money in fines. Working out of the Powerful was not natural to me, but I learned do this, as on many occasions I had to make decisions, move people quickly, and motivate others into action. These are strong traits of the Powerful.

My father was also a Powerful, and even though he was only in my life for the first ten years, his influence built into me an ease around operating from that quadrant.

Sometimes we have to step up and operate out of other quadrants, and find that we can. But to do that constantly will drain you.

Why not ask a colleague to do the profile on you? See if they see you as you see yourself. It's a great idea to get your team to do this, and then plot a table to show where everyone sits.

Playful	Powerful	Playful	Powerful
Peaceful	Precise	Peaceful	Precise

Playful	Powerful	Playful	Powerful
Peaceful	Precise	Peaceful	Precise

All too often, we get bogged down by the weaknesses of others. Focusing on this saps us of productivity and the enjoyment of what we do. Weaknesses are our strengths way out of balance, or pushed to extremes. This usually happens when there is stress, or when our needs aren't being met.

As a Playful, my ability to communicate is a strength. When does it become a weakness? When I over-talk, go off on tangents, speak louder to be heard, butt in and don't listen. These are all extremes of one of my strengths. To stop them becoming a weakness, I need to bring them into alignment.

Powerfuls are natural-born leaders and make things happen. Pushed to extremes, or out of balance, they become too bossy, domineering, autocratic, insensitive, impatient and unwilling to delegate or give credit to others.

The Precise are analytical, organised and logical. When operating out of their weaknesses, they spend too much time on preparation, get too focused on details, become pedantic, are disappointed in others and their performance and remember, and can dwell on, negatives.

Peacefuls are very good at listening, and are easy-going and non-confrontational. Pushed to extreme, they say little, put things off for another day, resist change and won't make decisions. You can see that operating out of their weaknesses might drive others crazy!

The next four chapters describe these four dominant personalities. Whichever primary personality you scored highest on, read that chapter first. Then read about your secondary.

Of course it's also worth your while to read about those who are very different from you. Often this will be your spouse, as we are often drawn to our opposite in relationships.

In each of these chapters we will qualify each personality type's strengths and weaknesses, what behaviours they display, their key drivers, how to present to them, how they frustrate others, and how you can get the best from them.

I will show you how to identify each type through clothing, gestures, voice tone and body language. By being able to identify this, if you are a leader or decision-maker, you will be able to place them in positions which will make them want to come to work every day.

Discovering who we are is wonderfully liberating. Discovering what others want is even better.

The Playful personality

5

Words describing the Playful
Highlight those words that describe you.

Animated	Vivacious	Enjoys new things
Encouraging	Energetic	Enthusiastic
Expressive	Friendly	Funloving
Generous	Outgoing	Loves variety
Motivator	Open	Playful
Promoter	Positive	Social
Takes chances	Talker	Forgiving

Because we can have characteristics from other personalities as well, these words may not exactly describe you, but if you are predominantly a Playful you will recognise many of them. There will be a lot of things in this chapter that you will be able to identify with, and, for those who work with a Playful, help you to understand what makes them tick. Personally, I find it easy to write about the Playful as this is my primary and instinctive personality!

Strengths
There is nothing quite like having a Playful on your team. They are great at motivating others. They bring energy and life into dull

and boring situations. Enthusiasm oozes from them, and they are naturally positive.

'Fun' is the best word to describe them. Because they love variety and flexibility, they don't mind starting and restarting a job. They can go off on tangents, but that is part of how they get the best possible outcome (if they come back to the issue at hand, that is).

They thrive in environments where they get to talk and have a vote on major decisions. They need to feel they are making a connection with whoever they're talking to. They want to build a rapport first, unafraid to ask questions that others would feel were too personal.

Talking is their very favourite pastime, and they would have a go at speaking on any subject, even if they didn't have any information about it. They usually talk until they know what they are saying! In fact, they talk like it's their last night on earth! They are certainly not afraid to put themselves 'out there'.

As a manager working with Playfuls, I always found it a good idea to ask these friendly folk first thing on a Monday morning what they did over the weekend, because if I didn't they'd tend to repeat themselves all day until someone listened and acknowledged them.

Their ego is the size of a small planet. It's like the little boy who wanted to play darts with this father and said, 'Come on, Dad, let's play darts. I'll throw, and you shout "wonderful!"'

They can come across as very confident people. Interestingly though, if you criticise them, they can withdraw right into a cave. They wilt under criticism and poor reviews. They are sensitive to disapproval, and spend their waking hours trying to win over that person they sense has no time for them.

They love people, and especially like meeting new ones. Probably because they have so many relationships, they often don't have the depth that others have. They are known to be fair-weather friends.

They are the ones who most often initiate contact. No one is ever a stranger, so Playfuls are in their element in front-line positions where they can connect with others. They flourish where there are people, and get their energy from being with them. Put them into a back room with only a computer and no people contact and it won't be long before they lose motivation.

What people in management love about these types is that they don't seem to bring yesterday's dramas into today. They very rarely carry a grudge, and are the most forgiving of all types. Why? Because they don't *remember* yesterday! They don't brood on what has happened. That is how they maintain a positive and cheery outlook.

They empty their 'thought' files each night. Everything's gone, forgotten. They love living in the moment, and look forward to what fun thing they can plan for tomorrow.

Playfuls bounce back from any setback or criticism very quickly — a valuable trait, especially when there is tension in the workplace. They remain buoyant and energetic, looking for the up-side in every situation. Always the encourager, these sociable beings prefer to work in a team where they can do just that. They love flexibility and variety and can despise the 'same old, same old'.

If they are wrong, they ask for forgiveness easily, or say 'sorry' even if it should be someone else that needs to say it. Others, particularly those who have a tendency to hold grudges, don't like how easy it is for Playfuls to say 'sorry' so sometimes they don't see it as truly genuine.

Of all the four personalities, Playfuls have the ability to look for the silver lining in every situation. We can all experience depression at some time in our life, but Playfuls have a strong ability to mask it. They can be sad on the inside, but on the outside they will still be able to laugh at life and be the fun person. In fact, when they are sad, or even quiet for that matter, you will hear others ask them, 'Why are you quiet? What's wrong?' It seems they aren't allowed to be this way, according to others!

These types work well under pressure, and rise to any challenge set before them, adjusting quickly to changing circumstances. They work at keeping things simple, and their appealing traits are inspirational and enthusiastic.

Weaknesses
When out of balance, Playfuls' strong love of people tends to get

them into all sorts of strife. Too much horsing around, neglecting priorities, getting distracted . . . the list goes on.

For instance, their time-management skills can become poor, resulting in a reputation for being late, overlooking deadlines and committing to things that are impossible to achieve. It's usually because they are over-committed or have agreed to too many things, therefore tasks remain unfinished. It's not that they *want* to be this way, they just get sidetracked. This is where the issues and tensions can start, both at work and at home.

When you get a Playful married to a Precise, for example, the Precise would regard attending one social engagement on Saturday night to be more than enough. The Playful, on the other hand, would want to move from one to several others. They don't like missing anything. A Precise would rather meet one or two people and relate on a deeper level, but you can't do that easily if you are flitting around.

If you ask a Playful to do an errand for you, expect them to take twice the anticipated time, as they get distracted easily. They might run into a friend while out, and get caught up in a long conversation. Because they are so 'in the moment' they overlook time, and before long they are running late.

Often, in business situations, these types can wear thin with others. They are perceived as loud, distracting, and 'Really, do they do any work?' — especially by the Precise, who loves to work where it's quiet. The Precise thinks, 'They can't possibly be working if they are talking!'

It's not uncommon for a Precise to berate a Playful about their management of time, or make strong suggestions about how they could do things differently. Playfuls tend to dart from one thing to another. They can walk into another office area, get distracted by something interesting and it's morning-tea time before they get back to their desk to deal with the issue they originally set out to overcome.

They have been known to tell stories at the expense of truth, and always embellish reality. It's not unusual for them to let their stories run away with them. If they have a group of people listening to their stories, they think, 'Well, why not add a bit here or there?' In time, they believe the exaggeration. They hardly know themselves what is true or untrue after a while.

Sadly, the Precise aren't impressed and, after rolling their eyes in exasperation, feel the need to correct them and show them up for who they are. It's not long before the Playfuls make a quick exit from those who disapprove of them.

In conversation they are such excitable, loud types that they tend to butt in, talk over others and change the subject, which can infuriate the other participants. When they don't get their needs met, they get even louder.

They are visual thinkers, so filing and being organised is something they can do, but they often put it off or place it at the bottom of the to-do list. Better that the document be left under the paperweight, than filed away. No sooner is it filed away, they're thinking, 'Where on earth did I file it?'

They can be frivolous, both in spending money and in conversation. Others may see them as shallow and superficial.

They avoid confrontation at all costs. Their greatest fear is loss of social acceptance and approval. That is how they get trapped into people pleasing, making sure they stay on everyone's good side. As social acceptance and approval are really big for them, they find it hard to be direct with people, so sometimes the hard issues are avoided.

These weaknesses are easily eradicated when you know what the Playful needs. When managing these types, you need to encourage them, and use the 'commend, recommend, commend' approach. Tell them what they have done well, get them to figure out what they could do better, and then commend them again. They will go all out for you if you do.

Visual clues
Clothing
Playfuls love colour and their clothing has to be stylish and vibrant (remember the lady in the airport lounge?). And yes, male Playfuls

love to be as eye-catching as the females — their ties or tie-pins and snappy logos on their socks are usually dead giveaways. They love colognes, perfumes, anything that will get them a compliment or be a conversation starter. Accessories are bold and distracting; anything that makes them visible

One example is a rather high-profile manager who often wears bright, outlandish shirts. This was best summed up by one of his colleagues, who said, 'That's not a shirt — it's a statement.' The shirt made a clear statement that he was a Playful type and of the confidence he had within himself.

James, my friend and colleague, shared a story with me about someone he was able to identify visually as a Playful: Jordan Luck, lead singer of The Exponents, and a successful New Zealand songwriter and entertainer. He is always heard from afar in bars and is a real showman on stage. In his younger days in Christchurch, when he was trying to make an impression in the entertainment industry, he could often be seen cutting a dashing figure in an old, Napoleon-type battle-dress jacket.

When they are walking down the street, it is apparent that Playfuls are observing their reflection in the window. It's not long before they are thinking to themselves, 'Man, do I look good!'

Gestures and body language
When trying to identify the different personalities, I would say Playfuls are the easiest to identify. Why? Because they seem to be the most open.

Even if they aren't speaking, their whole body is communicating. They use their hands as much as their mouths to get their message across. Their physical and facial gestures are very animated. The way they express themselves is bigger in every way than the other types — they are very 'high energy'.

Listen to laughter in any group, and you will probably hear and spot the Playful. They have the loudest belly laugh. It's a dead giveaway — and it's infectious. Every part of their body shakes when they laugh. It's entertaining to watch and they can captivate you for hours with their stories.

Their eyes also reveal who they are. They sparkle and are inviting — so it's no surprise that Playfuls can get themselves into the most trouble! They can be naive, however, and their actions can be misread by others. Their intention is just to connect and enjoy others.

They can't keep their hands to themselves, and have to touch to make a connection. When they meet you, it's not just a shake of the hand, but often a gentle touch on the arm or a hug. (In contrast, the Precise wouldn't even think of using a gentle touch on the first meeting. Perhaps a formal handshake, but that would be it. One has to earn the right with those more private types.)

Playfuls, however, just barge through that invisible personal-space barrier, and connect with a warm hug or lingering handshake. In a business situation, by the time the meeting is over, it's a hug rather than a handshake. This can leave non-Playful people confused as to how to respond. They wish Playfuls would adhere to simple business etiquette to stop the confusion!

Voice and tone

The Playful's voice tone and pitch match what they are saying, and they regularly change the inflection to hold people's attention. They usually speak at a rapid pace, with lots of emotion.

Playfuls are articulate and have great communication skills. They can get a point across to any audience, large or small. They just love to talk, and would certainly rather talk than listen.

You can hear these types before you see them, either singing to themselves as they walk up the pathway, or over everyone else's voice as they'll call out or invite someone to join them.

Whatever the situation they will bring or turn it towards fun.

Environment

Playfuls can also be easily identified through their environment, but they can trick you as well. Because of their need for social acceptance, they will do 'whatever it takes' to fit in — even tidying their office. But left to their own devices, they don't mind a mess. In fact, messy works for them.

At their work station you might see many group photos pinned

37

onto their walls, or a meaningful gift on display. Playfuls are energised with colour, so need to bring their artistic flair to the area where they work.

Stress

Playfuls are interesting when under stress, and have various ways of handling it.

Shopping is often what they resort to when stressed out. They find it great therapy. They have a preference for malls where there are lots of people, as they get their energy from this. However, after they shop they have major attacks of buyer's remorse when the credit card statement arrives — especially when their partner wants an explanation!

If they are attacked, they may cry, or charge back with a full defence. Their voice will be loud, to the extreme of shouting, and anyone in earshot will get 'a bit of their lip'.

The consolation with Playfuls is that they may blow up, but then it's usually finished, dealt with, over! They lay it down. If they have had an outburst they can be unaware of the debris of hurt left in their wake, so are sometimes seen by others as flippant.

It takes a lot to stress these Playfuls; as they have a strong need to be accepted, they would take it rather than give it. It's not uncommon for them, when caught between a rock and a hard place, to display a tendency to blame others.

I remember driving to work one day at about 5 a.m. I hit at least 60 kph in a 50 zone, only to be caught by the traffic officer. He proceeded to sternly lecture me, as well as write a speeding ticket, and all I could say was, 'What about that car passing me — you can't tell me he was going 50!' Blaming others in an attempt to squirm out of the situation is a trait you will see mostly with Playfuls.

They are the type most prone to emotional eating, so when they're stressed, it's 'down the hatch' before you know it. Then there's the continual battle of weight loss. Any weight-loss programme that promotes counting calories or points is out: they forget half the time what has gone into their mouths.

When it comes to stress-related diseases, like the Powerful, these types can blow their fuses. This can cause high blood pressure, strokes and heart attacks. They need to manage their stress according to their personality.

Work

They are happy-go-lucky types, and as long as there is fun in the workplace, these people will put in the hours and effort. They love prestige and recognition, so aren't afraid of work to get this.

Planning

The Playful can't help themselves volunteering for things, and usually end up overselling their ability and being overcommitted. They love to be in on everything, and find focusing on just one thing boring, so up goes their hand, time and time again. They wonder how on earth they are going to finish all they said they would. Usually they don't.

Leadership

In summary, the Playful is an inspirational leader. They have a bounty of charisma, and are great motivators, endlessly encouraging and never failing to cheer their team on.

Meetings

These types are not afraid to speak up. They communicate well, but can go off on tangents if they don't have an agenda in front of them. Rather than relate details and facts, they will give a metaphor or tell a story that gets the point across. They are apt to change the subject and could do this many times during the meeting.

They are easily distracted, and need to exercise real discipline to stay on course with something as laborious as details. Playfuls are not prone to reading long notes, small print and detailed documents, but they are great ideas people, and love to brainstorm and bounce ideas around.

They don't care for formal meetings and prefer cafés and

restaurants to conduct business meetings, where they can draw their energy from the surrounding activity. They think better in these situations.

Decision-making

Playfuls make decisions intuitively on what it all feels like to them on the day, using that indescribable 'instinct' which seems for the most part to work. They tend to be impulsive and buy in quickly to what has been presented without doing their homework, and also have a tendency to go with the crowd. Often the Playful acts in haste and then has to find ways to recover. They are led by their heart and emotions.

Presenting

Playfuls will work at relationship-building prior to presenting. They can charm the gatekeepers into divulging names and positions held to assist them in their presentation.

They are very polished and charming, so are highly persuasive, innovative, enthusiastic and optimistic, and engage their audience quickly.

Playfuls can turn it on even under pressure. They can 'wing it' and think quickly on their feet, and can see and deliver simple solutions. They prefer to avoid the discipline of preparation. If other issues are brought up, Playfuls quickly latch onto them with great enthusiasm, and get excited about them. They sometimes like to get to the results before presenting the whole picture.

They are good at presenting in words and pictures that can powerfully tell the story. Their spontaneous responses engage their audience more than their elaborate explanations.

When presenting to a Playful, be enthusiastic, warm, interested and fascinated. Show a personal interest and get them to talk about themselves. Building relationships is most important to these types. Keep business-related questions precise.

Playfuls' love of brainstorming and being as creative as possible can detract from the issues at hand. They can get caught up in the outcomes without hearing all the facts and important information.

Because they aren't into detail and small print, they may have to come back round to what was being talked about before sign-off or a decision is made. When you ask them about the big picture, though, they can describe it eloquently.

The important key in dealing with a Playful is that they need to see the benefits. Don't present in a complicated way. Do the paperwork and details for them.

They warm to people who give them the liberty and independence to choose and to experience, and who allow them flexibility. But most importantly, they warm to someone who really makes an effort with them.

Emails

The following is an example of how a Playful would send an email invitation to a meeting.

Dear Jennie,

You have no idea how great it feels that I can be out of the office and know things are ticking over nicely in my absence. I am sure you are entertaining everyone with those eventful happenings in your life. :-)

It seems ages since we have caught up. I feel like I have been in a plane for the whole month of October. It's been interesting, though, and there have been so many incidents, I am considering writing a book about them all! Perhaps I will share them when I next see you. Let me tell you just one. When I got to my destination, I picked up a suitcase identical to mine and, horror of horrors, when I opened it at the hotel, I find it's full of children's Christmas presents . . . I didn't know whether to take my make-up off, in case they couldn't locate my bag before the next working day!

Enough of that. You'll be pleased to know that I have had some great feedback from our clients regarding how focused you are on the project.

I hope you are encouraged by the results at this point. I am.

Looking forward to our meeting next week, when we can have

a discussion on how far we've come and determine what the next phase is.

In fact, because we have worked so hard, as a small way of saying thank you I will arrange for my PA to get some nibbles and drinks in on this occasion (party time!). So please note this will be at 4.30 p.m. next Monday 3rd November. I am writing that in my diary this very minute.

Looking forward to seeing you all.

Susan

P.S. Enclosed by attachment is a hilarious joke that was sent to me, you may enjoy it.

Relating socially

These types will do just about anything to have a social get-together. They will go 'hammer and tongs' at a task if they know there is a reward like a social gathering at the end. Their fun and energy will lift the spirits of a group and bring light to the darkest of moods.

Because they would rather talk than listen, they can gather around them an assortment of those who prefer to listen. Their 'little disasters' get visited and re-visited, and they cleverly weave an adventure into telling the story. It won't be too long before you hear someone say, 'Tell us more about that . . . '

They love seeking out others, and are not afraid to initiate contact. If they are involved with organising a function, they may forget their other tasks but will always volunteer for the 'meet and greet' job. Tidying up afterwards can be a huge effort for them.

They are great networkers and are comfortable with crowds.

Today the big buzzword is social intelligence. Playfuls far exceed all other personalities in this quotient.

If you want to relate to a Playful, make sure you emphasise the importance of people. To them, personal relationships aren't beside the point, they *are* the point, and this will be very important in their ongoing association with you.

Key drivers

Included in the Playful's toolbox is the ability to maintain energy and enthusiasm when the going gets tough. They have stacks of it. Conversations with them are, more often than not, stimulating.

Playfuls are your creative types who excel at thinking up new activities and ideas. Their spontaneity is refreshing. Fun is their favourite word, and therefore they like to gear everything towards that.

Their ability to inspire those who struggle is a great strength to have on a team. Their preference is giving a report in person, rather than in writing, because of their strong belief in themselves. Being able to convince others to take a risk is always an asset.

These are our 'live for today', 'seize the moment', 'trust in your dreams' types. They love the panic of life. They create it with their over-commitment to activity.

People come first. They love them and can't work without them. Playfuls are warm, friendly and responsive. They gravitate to other people, so it's not uncommon to see them lured to someone's desk and starting a conversation. They are not afraid to initiate conversation, so in the area of sales, they are good at getting new clients and at relationship building. They are very good networkers and have a wide circle of contacts.

You can find these optimistic characters in books written about prisoner-of-war camps. The Playful is always the encourager, inspiring the discouraged in the camp to 'hold on — liberation is closer than it's ever been.' Transfer that into the workplace and you will have on your team someone who can break the tensions in a light and humorous way.

Playfuls flourish and blossom in an active, buzzing environment, and love working in a team coming up with new ideas. The application and delivery of these ideas can be another matter, however.

Because they have charisma to burn, Playfuls gravitate to roles in business such as sales, speakers, presenters, networkers, front line — anywhere they can be at the centre of the activity. They love to be where they can help people.

These types are great at promoting people or projects. They

naturally default to communication, media and publicity roles, where they can use their quick thinking and not be at the same desk, day in and day out.

They would rather talk than work, but are happy to put their ability to talk to work. If you want to get the best out of them, put them with people and give them a multiplicity of activity focusing on fun.

The Playful is so valuable in the workplace and at home, as they bring so much energy, enthusiasm and life. Give them *attention, affection, approval* and *acceptance,* and you will have on your team an extraordinary player who will get the work done and bring humour and creativity.

6 The Precise personality

Words describing the Precise
Highlight those words that describe you.

Calculating	Classic	Critical thinker
Cool and calm	Deliberate	Detailed
Exacting	Factual	Fastidious
High ideals	Intentional	Logical
Loves the arts	Tidy	Persistent
Practical	Predictable	Objective
On time	Reserved	Well-mannered

Because we can have characteristics from other personalities as well, these words may not exactly describe you, but if you are predominantly a Precise you will recognise many of them and there will be a lot of things in this chapter that you will be able to identify with. If you work with a Precise, this chapter will help you to understand what pushes their buttons.

Strengths
Precise types are thoughtful, logical, well-mannered, persistent and fact-based.

They have a natural instinct to probe and research. They value any role that requires accurate planning and detail, usually setting a goal and working back from it (the only type that does this).

They require facts and more facts, which they carefully analyse before making their final conclusion. This is most interesting to observe in action. They probe and question until they clearly know what is required of them, checking to make sure everything is right. The Precise has a fetish for accuracy and craves data. I find it really hard to think like that, but for these types, it's natural.

They are known to be the most intellectual of all four types, because they go below the surface, always inquiring and digging for more information, and seeking evidence. They are excellent at staying on task, and can see all sides of an issue. Precises love the depths of life and their exacting skills make them respected by their peers.

Because of their logical thinking habits, they have a tendency to make decisions rationally and factually, and can separate themselves emotionally from the process. Their astute critical skills are used to achieve the desired outcomes.

The Precise is more of a historian than a futurist. Their focus is on past experiences and the subsequent need to refine their actions. They always want to know the down-side to everything that *could* go wrong, and sometimes that can come across as negative. Not that they would see it like that — they would argue that they just want to make sure they have their bases covered, and that there will be no surprises.

They are sticklers for details. Their eyes are like scanners and can spot errors within moments, often seeing mistakes others don't. They set high standards for themselves — and for others. They abhor making errors and cringe when others make them. Their motto would be 'Measure twice, cut once'.

These are the types who get exasperated when others don't finish things, or don't put away what needs to be put away. When they are frustrated by others, they won't say anything, but sigh, tsk or shake their heads. Their body language speaks loudly when they are annoyed. There are no words to express how agonising they find it when others make mistakes!

Aren't you glad that most of our engineers and specialist doctors are Precise personalities? Can you imagine a Playful opening you up? They would have an organ resting in the palm of their hand and say, 'Now, where did this come from? Oh well, not a problem!' and discard it! While these types won't have the bedside manner of a Playful, be thankful they are Precise. Put up with their self-contained and cool manner because they will get the job done, and done well. Despite outward appearances, they are very compassionate people, and can suffer internally.

Precise types have a strong sense of justice and fair play. They adhere to strict moral codes, and have a strong social conscience. They care deeply for the planet, and are compassionate towards the less privileged. They are fair and reasonable in their approach to issues and challenges, but can be black and white.

I remember once telling a Precise a joke. After the punchline, his expression was unchanged. I said, 'That was funny!' He said, 'I know.' I said, 'Why aren't you laughing?' He said, 'I am!' I discovered that day that Precises laugh internally!

They tend to labour over cause and effect before putting themselves forward to debate something. Precises tend to be shy about making big claims, and are measured in what they say and how they say it.

A Precise came up to me after a training session and asked me, 'Since we are having a second session with this particular group, should I keep my name card?' These people are thrifty and frugal — great savers of everything. 'Work before play' is another of their mottoes, and they strictly adhere to timeframes.

A Precise I know went on a business trip to Australia, a two-hour time difference from his home. He phoned his wife and said he had been out until 1.30 a.m. She was surprised, as he's not one to stay out late, but then he commented, 'New Zealand time, of course.'

The next day he phoned and said he was having dinner, and she was surprised again when he said it was only 5 p.m. local time. 'You never eat at five,' she said. 'Oh,' he replied, 'I have kept to New Zealand time so I'm not out of sync when I get back.'

Only a Precise would do such a thing. Very logical and practical. It made sense to him!

Their intensity and deep love of life equates to appreciation of the fine arts, music and the environment, far more than the other types. They can be theatrical, stepping out of their comfort zones to go into character, but then reverting to their quiet stance.

They are very caring and loving people, but others have to earn the right to see this side of them. It is not given at first meeting.

Weaknesses

The very thing that makes these types brilliant can also be their biggest weakness. When out of balance or taken to extremes, their ability to organise, get things done in a systematic way and think logically can come across as nit-picky, pedantic and prone to perfectionism. They so want to get things done right that they have a tendency to spend too much time in preparation, which can result in procrastination.

They don't understand others who would like to play as they work. For the Precise, play is a reward for *after* the work is done.

Precises have been known to look down on 'dummies' and make others feel less intelligent. They don't intentionally try to do this or actually feel more intelligent; it is due to their desire for correctness and deep thinking which can alienate others trying to engage with them.

Precise types find it hard to be generous with praise. Because of their high ideals, they always think there is room for improvement, hence they hold back in giving it.

In the workplace, it's not uncommon to see signs in the lunchroom saying 'Please do your own dishes — we are not your mother', usually written by a Precise. They love writing notes like this. They may also comment in a stern way when you borrow a pencil, 'Make sure you bring it back as soon as you are done with it'. They will issue all sorts of instructions, as they feel the need to enforce some order.

Because they are so cautious, they have a tendency to be suspicious of others. They certainly wouldn't take people at face value. 'Prove yourself first' is another catchphrase.

In meetings, they can be seen as the dampeners of ideas. That isn't their intention, but they like to know the down-sides and have a tendency to want to discuss them.

They have sharp minds, and can remember when someone has slighted or offended them, which can result in long-term persecution and a tendency to be short on forgiveness. They find it hard to let go of things.

Their mind works for them, giving them the ability to set and achieve goals. It also works against them, their high ideals limiting their joy and making them agonise when they make an error, beating themselves up for days.

I asked a Precise how they thought they might irritate others, and they responded that they:

- seem obsessive-compulsive
- seem tense, edgy or anally retentive
- correct others' wrongs; if things aren't finished or done properly, others get to hear about it
- seem negative
- are too structured and one-eyed
- are too tidy and too persistent
- could sound critical, and
- tend to respond to questions with details and facts.

Visual clues
Clothing
Precise types love 'state-of-the-art' everything. They are strongly classic in their clothing preferences, tending towards straight lines and more formal looks. Top-shelf quality is preferred — they would rather have two very well-made suits than six run-of-the-mill.

Now here's a paradox: some Precises prefer the eclectic look — hippie, grunge or alternative — eye-catching in an intriguing way. They don't care to look like a mass-produced person, and search in the most unusual places for things that are different. They can err on the side of being unorthodox. These Precises are more interested in the inner person than the outer incidentals.

Gestures and body language

The body language of the Precise is more closed than that of the other types. By that I mean you can't read these people easily. They are private, self-contained people, who don't gesture much. They love to work alone, preferably where it's quiet. They are very emotionally restrained — definitely not the huggy, chummy type (only to those close to them who have earned the right). They respect each other's distance and personal space, and hope others respect theirs.

It's difficult to read their faces and body language. Every thought is kept well hidden, but they are constantly evaluating what is going on. Each gesture is deliberately thought out. They walk more slowly than Powerfuls and Playfuls.

Voice and tone

Precises speak at a controlled pace, displaying limited emotion and enthusiasm. The volume is low, with little inflection, and they may seem cautious and non-committal in manner.

They usually don't speak until they know what they really need to say. When communicating with them, it's easy to imagine them formulating a response, scanning their minds for the right words. Interestingly though, if you find a connection with these people through a hobby or interest, you can't stop them talking.

In conversation, they might pause as they put their words together perfectly. This can cause a lot of frustration for the other types, especially the Powerful, as they try to jump in on the pauses, but if they try they will get a strong disapproving look.

The Precise has a need to explain everything in full, factual, consecutive order, to the point of saying, 'Jeff replied . . . and I said . . . and then he said . . . She interjected and said . . .'

They really can paint a picture for you — and equally, drive you crazy as you sit through their monologues.

If you have a Precise boss, they will want all the information before you set out on a task. Sometimes that can frustrate the employee with all their questioning: 'Where are you going?', 'How long are you going to be?', 'Who will you be with?', 'What time can I expect you to be finished?', 'Are those other things really important?', 'Do you really need all this information?'

You can interpret this as they don't trust you. Misunderstandings can easily take place, when all they are really doing is getting the information they need so they can plan and organise the next phase of what needs doing.

I thought my husband distrusted me for years, the way he asked all these questions. Little did I realise that he was asking me so that when I returned home, I would find the outside light on, the garage door up, a hot-water bottle in bed, and a hot milky drink waiting for me! How did I not see that?

The following email was sent to me by a Precise. It explains what they are like far better than I could. They favour the written word above the spoken, well thought-through and well written.

Each year around this time (almost like clockwork), I've happened to spot a pair of ducks (male and female) stopping off in our pool on their migration. I've only seen them one day each year and only for a few minutes so I've been lucky to spot them each year. I suppose they could come some other day but I doubt it. I know the times because the photos on my digital camera retain the time taken. I'm not sure if they are the same pair but I suspect they are. Interesting that they choose to use our pool. This year we had to drain the pool to have the liner repaired and it was totally empty, until we had about seven days of rainwater collect in the bottom —just in time for their return. Sometimes nature can be quite amazing — even in the city.

You can see how detail is important to the Precise. That's why when they don't get it right and make mistakes they beat themselves up for a long time after. After meetings they will conduct a mental post mortem on every conversation that took place.

Environment
Because of their insatiable need to be organised, they have very orderly work stations with only one project at a time on their desk

and everything else filed neatly away in colour-coded reference sections. It's not unusual for them to have charts and graphs up on the walls, or their credentials, which sends out a strong message: respect my intellectual bias, as I have worked for it and done the hard yards.

Their environment is more formal and minimalist than that of the other types. They prefer to work alone, as they find noise a distraction. They will often have their doors closed to the world, quietly working away.

You can spot Precise people in the workplace, because they are usually cleaning up (after the cleaner). They have a fetish for order and tidiness. If the cleaner has put their paperweight down in the wrong place, they will leave a little note telling them not to do it again! They are always on time for work, and know when others aren't.

Stress

The Precise has the greatest propensity to worry and internalise things. They have a great ability to recall information, but this means they can create a lot of stress for themselves as they play mental gymnastics, interpreting and sometimes misinterpreting what others have said and done. This can be totally draining. Often they can become depressed, and pull away and withdraw for long periods. They would rather do this than have to respond in any emotional way.

They can never work out why others don't see things the way they see them. Because they hold on to issues and things that have slighted them, they find forgiving difficult. Sadly, they can't see that this destroys them more than it does the offender. Learning to apply the old-fashioned virtue of forgiveness can help Precises take life less seriously. And they need to practise forgiveness of themselves first.

Their high standards can cause them to fall under a black cloud. The Precise needs to understand that we don't live in a perfect world, so 'good' is good enough. They want perfection, but this will end up destroying them if they constantly refuse to accept anything less.

Precise, it's OK to make mistakes. We learn through them. Don't beat yourself up. There are plenty of others who would like to do that!

Because of their tendency to internalise, these types can suffer from the 'worry' diseases such as depression, skin irritations, food reactions etc.

Work
Planning
The Precise have a tendency to over-plan. They love organising and scheduling, work hard at being on time, prefer a tidy workplace and give correct information, backed with heaps of data. This can throw their time management out the window, because they spend more time on research and planning and not enough on execution. They can become overwhelmed by all that needs to be achieved, then procrastinate.

Leadership
The Precise's leadership style is strategic. This is born out of their ability to organise well. They also have brilliant critical skills and a deep creativity.

As leaders they are sensitive to people's feelings but demand quality.

Meetings
Precise people come to meetings well prepared. They will stay up half the night to get things ready.

Because they have strong critical skills, they are prepared to put their neck on the line. Their critical nature can be seen as negative, but in many instances, because they can see the downside of situations, they help the group deal with issues that might otherwise be overlooked. They can be sceptical until all the data has been presented.

They do their research on the latest gizmos and high-tech products well before others get wind of them, and then can be seen using them. They like the fact that people inquire and show interest, asking them about their new toy and what it can do for them.

It can be frustrating to others how much information they love to give. When asked to present, there will be nothing they miss out.

They probably won't talk much in a meeting, observing, thinking and being cautious, having to try things out for size before commenting. They mentally record every conversation, so they won't be caught giving the wrong information.

Not strongly entrepreneurial, they are more concrete, tried-and-true, objective types. They go with their head and logic rather than their heart and how they feel.

After the meeting they will comment on how exhausted they are. Being with people for too long drains them.

Decision-making

Precises prefer to gather data first, using their critical skills to dig out anything that could possibly go wrong. They will only make decisions based on well-researched data that has been tested and proven.

Common sense and logic are used to process most things. They are not afraid to debate something if they feel strongly about it, and they stand up against moral injustices.

Presenting

Their personal presentation is immaculate, and they love formal introductions and protocols. Precises are more interested in developing a professional relationship than a personal one.

They favour the written word. Those attending one of their presentations will probably receive written information about what's coming.

Their love for words can cause them to talk longer than most presenters, providing methodical and complex information backed up with graphs, charts and reputable evidence. They will be deliberate in showing how things can be done or how they can be achieved with costs and timeframes considered.

When presenting to a Precise, use impeccable manners. Be mindful that they favour the written word, and that they require more detail and could ask a lot more questions than any other type.

They want exact figures, not rough estimates, and they don't like quick fixes, or solutions that haven't been examined properly. The Precise will be turned off if you do not know your product well.

Precises want references — to know what experts have to say — and will do their homework. They will make a deliberate and thoughtful decision after weighing up the pros and cons. They want comparisons and established evidence.

They seek to know *how*: How did you reach that conclusion? How much will it cost? How will we work this through? How will this impact on my bottom line? How much research have you put into this? How can we sharpen the pencil? . . . the list goes on.

Emails

The following is an example of how a Precise would send an email invitation to a meeting:

Dear Jennie,

I am looking forward to getting back to the office and hearing what's been happening while I have been away.

You will have already received the agenda regarding our planned meeting sent out on 28th October 2006. I am sure you have already noted this in your diary.

I am counting on full attendance. If for some reason you cannot attend, I would appreciate an immediate response and preferably the reason why.

Because I am concerned with the volume of items that need to be covered, I am asking everyone to make a concerted effort to be there on time.

In order that we all come prepared I have enclosed by attachment charts and graphs of last month's results which will give you an idea of where we sit as we plan and strategise the next phase.

It is self-explanatory, but if there is anything you are unsure about, I would prefer it if you would speak to me before the meeting, so we can maximize our time together and get through the agenda.

I have allocated each person five minutes to feedback to the team their challenges over the past month. I am particularly interested in how you have overcome these challenges.

Warmest regards

Jon

Relating socially

When there is a work social occasion, these types do it more out of duty than desire. In my travels, at business functions I have often found a few stray Precise types marking time in the washrooms with their glass of wine, willing the time to pass quicker. They are prepared to meet their company's expectation to attend, but they would much rather be at home with those they really care about and love.

Their social graces are impeccable. They have outstanding table manners and show courtesies. Always remember to send a note of thanks after any event they put on.

The Precise are sensitive to other people's needs, as well as needing people to be sensitive to theirs. This can mean there are strings attached to any relationship.

They remember dates and special celebrations, and can feel hurt when others don't take the time or effort to do the same. Their caring and compassionate nature makes them empathetic listeners, motivated to help.

Don't misunderstand the Precise: they can have fun, as long as their work is completed. It will prey on their mind if it's not.

Key drivers

The Precise have the ability to qualify and quantify everything, so fewer mistakes are made. They feel secure supported by structure and data, and it's hard for them to accept that others don't look at things the same way.

They have a love of analysis, and plan and organise well. They have a passion for scheduling and establishing processes and procedures.

Their strategic ability to save costs, crunch numbers and make a profit makes them valuable in the workplace. Precises have such a good eye for what could go wrong that they come well prepared to meetings. They stand up for injustices, so when there is a perceived offence they will feel deeply for the victim.

They are also great trainers, as they give clear instructions and explain everything well.

Give Precise personalities *space, silence, sensitivity* and *support* and you will have an employee or colleague who will contribute hugely to your team.

7 The Peaceful personality

Words describing the Peaceful
Highlight those words that describe you.

Approachable	Avoids conflict	Accepting
Balanced	Calming	Dislikes change
Dry humour	Easy-going	Good listener
Level-headed	Likes routine	Loyal
Mediator	Nurturing	Patient
Reliable	Relaxed	Steady
Tolerant	Understanding	Willing

Because we can have characteristics from other personalities as well, these words may not exactly describe you, but if you are predominantly a Peaceful you will recognise many of them and there will be a lot of things in this chapter that you will be able to identify with. If you work with a Peaceful, this chapter will help you understand what motivates them.

Strengths
These types are very reliable, versatile and a great support. They are brilliant listeners and are able to put things in context, therefore bringing clarity to any situation and integrating the past, present

and future. Their biggest strength is bringing order out of chaos, as they seek harmony.

Peacefuls function systematically and efficiently. They are great administrators and enjoy paperwork and routine. Very relaxed and pleasant people, they make no demands to be in the limelight or in pivotal positions of power. That's not to say they can't lead, but they would rather not.

There's nothing like having a Peaceful around when the heat is on. Very balanced types, they don't experience the highs and lows of life. Controlled and patient, they have a calming effect on others. Don't we need one of these on the team?

They take time to consider things, and are measured in their approach. Peacefuls like to problem-solve and have a compelling desire to finish tasks.

They value people more than goals, and even in leadership roles they are very supportive and nurturing. In fact, they can be preferred over the other types as leaders or supervisors as they are non-confrontational. And let's face it, when we spend 40-plus hours a week at work, isn't it a pleasure when there is minimal conflict? Peacefuls are prepared to work hard and finish the most menial tasks. They are great at keeping people happy and are gracious with small talk.

Peacefuls are internally strong — externals do not affect them. They love being in a team environment. They are very approachable sorts, and make an effort to focus on the positive aspects of people. Peacefuls are tolerant and accepting of others, and people like working with them.

Those with Peaceful personalities have a tendency to seek mediation positions, and are very good at them. They can easily sit on the fence and not take sides, because of their strong need for harmony. They are also good in areas such as counselling and mediation because they have a wonderful ability to hide their own feelings. They give nothing away and, because they listen so well, they can see what others don't.

Peacefuls are a paradox in that they don't like change but are adaptable. They don't like change because more often than not they are not given the reason why. Other personalities don't have the same intense desire to know this, but once you give it to Peacefuls, they will do whatever needs to be done.

You don't get dramas with these types. They are 'cruisers' and don't over-react, taking everything in their stride. 'Don't worry, be happy!' is a slogan of theirs.

They need time to think about things. I have purposely listed this as a strength, because while this can drive others absolutely nuts, their hesitancy to make instant decisions can be a great attribute when there are big decisions to be made. It gives everyone time to process the implications. As long as they are aware of when the decision has to be made, and why, they will embark on the process of making it.

Working with these types, you'll quickly find out that you can't push them or goad them into action. Just try and see how resistant they are!

They are fiercely loyal, open, sincere and faithful, and enjoy processes.

Weaknesses

As mentioned earlier, Peacefuls are hesitant to make quick decisions or speak up when they could or should. Here is the dichotomy. I have mentioned this as one of their strengths, but it can be seen by others as indecisiveness and non-engagement, and from where they stand it is a weakness. It can frustrate certain types, especially the Powerful.

Leave them to tackle things at their own pace ('Did anyone ever say it was a race?'). They prefer to digest information and *then* they will rise to the occasion, but if they are pushed or forced, that's when they show their colours. They dig in in a passive, procrastinating way. I'm telling you, you can't make these people do something they don't want to do!

Time is not of the essence for these people. They consider time to be on their side.

Their tendency to be internally strong can also be seen as a weakness. You could say they can be stubborn. They may seem to be walk-overs, but they are not push-overs. They will say, 'Don't take advantage of benevolence!' If push comes to shove, or if you try to drive these people too hard, they will finally come out like angry bulls, which confuses everyone, as the anger might seem to be over the slightest issue.

They work hard at keeping everyone happy. They would rather suppress conflict than resolve it, which means others have to work harder at solving the issues. Interestingly, Peacefuls actually manipulate and control through diplomacy and procrastination.

As relationships are most important to a Peaceful, good relationships equal wholehearted support from them. Don't ask them to take sides in a conflict between two parties; they will just support both sides after the issue has been dealt with (whether it has been dealt with correctly or not).

They can be too laid back at times and want to keep things the way they are. Others would call this avoidance, but they would say, 'Procrastination is the art of keeping up with yesterday.'

Peacefuls can be very selfish, choosing to do what they want in a very discreet way.

Visual clues
Clothing
Because Peacefuls are not affected by externals, they don't necessarily put a lot of emphasis on what they wear. Usually it's comfortable: trainers or comfortable shoes are the key piece in their wardrobe! They would be the most conservative of all the personalities in terms of dress, and put the least amount of energy into their presentation style.

Sometimes the extreme types can look as if they have just got out of bed, with their hair tousled and windswept and with very little definition.

Gestures and body language

It is hard to identify Peacefuls through gestures alone. Their movements are fluid, their gestures measured. It can be easy to spot them, though — leaning against the wall. Their thinking is, 'Why stand when you can sit? Why sit when you can lie down?'

When they sit down they flop, and usually stretch back and lean on an elbow. They often don't stand as erect as others. This is because they are great energy conservationists. Work interrupts their sleep. Don't get me wrong: they work hard, but their reward is rest. That's what motivates them. They like a time in their day when they literally do nothing.

They have the same facial expression whether they are happy, sad, angry or excited.

These types are very relational, so you see them walk quietly into a room and sit among the crowd, enjoying the conversation but never drawing attention to themselves. They are very comfortable with eye contact and very accepting in manner.

Voice and tone

Of all the personalities, Peacefuls are the most balanced. Therefore, you will find their speech has the same pitch for every conversation. They are softly spoken.

A Peaceful can have you hanging on every word as they slowly tell you a story, with lots of pauses and dry wit. These people are funny but in the driest of ways.

They might have you bowled off your seat, splitting your sides, but they are in the same position and show no emotion. They conserve energy in everything, so you can count on them to be the same yesterday, today and tomorrow. Their favourite word is 'whatever'.

Environment

Because the Peaceful do not go to extremes, they don't tend to stand out. Although it wouldn't be uncommon for them to have a photo of their family on their desk, some wouldn't go to that much trouble. They love keepsakes, so could possibly have something like this sitting in pride of place to trigger conversation — any old relic or piece of memorabilia that is of interest to them.

In my visits to different offices, I have found some interesting examples of this, for instance a beautiful piece of greenstone placed on their desk, or an historical article they have found (a sawn-off part of a musket, or some golden gum from the Northland gumfields). Peacefuls do have interests and hobbies, and those interests can consume them. Finding what interests them is the key that will seal a great relationship.

Stress

Because the Peaceful is not affected greatly by external factors, it takes a lot to get them stressed. They are the most adaptable, therefore can work in any environment, even under pressure. They are our 'steadies' when all else is falling apart. Their need is harmony and peace above all, and they will go to great lengths to keep the peace.

Working with them, we need to know, though, that when push comes to shove, these people can absolutely surprise you with their strong will. They have a tenacity beyond measure. They would rather not exert it, but oh, if they have to, they will.

Most often they avoid tensions as much as possible and usually withdraw and pull away. That's their way of saying, 'Something is wrong, talk to me about it.' Those they have taken into their confidence must listen with understanding, without interruption or justification, or the issue will get worse.

How they handle stress is either by dodging the bullets flying overhead, or hiding. A sure giveaway is getting lost in watching TV, and eating can also be a helpful distraction.

Work

Peacefuls find it difficult to anticipate how long a task will take and to work out what is most important. Clear instructions about the level of importance of a task help a Peaceful. Too many demands from too many people confuse them, and there needs to be one person they can go to who can help them prioritise in times like this.

Their strength, though, is that they will complete all tasks. You will be amazed sometimes how much they can get done in an hour. Their best work is often done under pressure, although this does exhaust them, and too much pressure will drive them away.

Peacefuls like doing the difficult or boring things at the beginning of the day and leaving the easier things to the end (work now, play later — unsupervised).

In a team environment where all are required to do the same work, when other members take advantage of the Peaceful's habits and leave the difficult things to the end of the day, this can aggravate the Peaceful, making them feel undervalued.

Peacefuls *need* to be appreciated. It's too easy to take advantage of a Peaceful because they always do what is required of them. Specific thanks goes a long way — not just 'thanks' but 'thank you for . . . ' The Powerful/Playful need to acknowledge the input of the Peaceful that has made them look good, and not just take all the glory themselves.

Peacefuls don't like being 'cornered' (e.g. don't ask them, 'What are you doing?' then dive in, saying, 'Well, can you do this for me now?') They like to please and will make allowances for everyone and everything, regardless of how busy they are. They need to be respected. A better way to phrase the above would be, 'When you've got time, would you mind doing this for me, I need it by . . . '

They are relaxed about time, preferring to deliver 'last minute' rather than early. But they will work beyond the call of duty to complete something.

They are quick learners when shown how to do something. They are eager to please and therefore learn quickly. This can be a real advantage in new situations.

Peacefuls are invaluable under pressured circumstances. They have a calming influence on everyone and, if left to do the task, are reliable.

They dislike too many deadlines or goals (other than normal weekly/daily deadlines). Keep these to a minimum. Peacefuls are irritated by people who demand too many things, too often, at the last minute (but of course would never show it).

Peacefuls are happy to be 'in the background' but don't like being ignored. They like feeling that they are a valuable part of a team. They like their role to be acknowledged as being important to the company or overall vision.

They feel that little 'insignificant' jobs are actually as important as big public events, for without the first there could be none of the second!

If a Peaceful expresses to you their dislike of something within the workplace — a person or task — this needs to be taken seriously. For other personalities, this is a simple statement. But to a Peaceful, this is confrontation. To express a dislike is major for them and takes all the courage they can muster.

Respect their dislikes and work towards a mutual compromise and you will gain a loyal employee. Ignore them and you will find they start talking to others about the issue (this is not seen by them as gossip, but a cry for help: 'Someone please help me solve this issue!') or, one day, your quiet, accepting Peaceful will explode or quit.

Don't mistake their lack of enthusiasm as lack of initiative. A Peaceful will use their initiative in a quiet, unassuming way.

Unless we understand personalities, Peacefuls can be misunderstood because of their low-key approach.

Planning
Peacefuls are likely to under-commit — they do not want to be laden down with more than is necessary, so resist volunteering for extra projects and taking on new tasks. They'll get their job done in their own time — not yours. If you push them, they will go even slower.

Leadership
Their leadership style is strongly diplomatic, gracious and restorative. They keep calm, are not impulsive, and so are well liked and inoffensive.

Peacefuls make excellent 2ICs. Give them responsibility and they'll come up with the goods. But they don't like the buck stopping with them, and make sure not too many responsibilities are piled on them (being the 'yes' people they are). Ensure the load is evenly distributed among the team.

Meetings

Usually a listener at meetings, the Peaceful's opinions are sought, as they can bring tremendous clarity and insight because of their ability to observe. They will only share their opinions in a comfortable environment and need to be acknowledged for their input and the validity of their idea (even if it is not adopted). They need to feel that their opinion has been properly considered, not brushed off or ridden over by another's opinion.

Too many opinionated people and too many disagreements will make a Peaceful remain uncomfortably silent. If a decision has been made without their inclusion, they will be slow to support it. Also, they will not buy in to or physically engage with a scheme if the reasons why it has been implemented aren't explained.

They are not assertive, so will very rarely challenge any issues where conflict is likely.

Decision-making

Peacefuls don't like making 'on-the-spot decisions', but given time to weigh up the pros and cons, they usually make good choices. Under pressure, they can be very indecisive and sometimes make bad decisions. When this happens it can be a cause of much frustration and make them feel angry, eating at their self-esteem.

As a manager, you need to respect the Peaceful's need for time; say, 'Can you let me know by . . .' rather than demanding an immediate decision.

When making decisions, the Peaceful will often ask various people what they would do — not for gossip's sake, but to help them consider different perspectives.

They would prefer to let things sit, and can therefore readily put things off for another day if they sense there is going to be any tension.

They anticipate and are prepared to address any ramifications and things that could go wrong, but they like to have thought before acting and to have things in context. They prefer the 'tried and true', and security rates highly for them.

The Peaceful will happily change to please, but if too many changes are required, the Peaceful will stop co-operating, especially if they have not been included in the discussion of why and how. They really feel taken advantage of when they hear something second-hand, so involve them in decision-making.

Presenting

Peacefuls will want to build a relationship first, and are very good at drawing others out. They prefer to take a more open, collaborative, relaxed approach — a dialogue — rather than doing it all.

They are modest and unassuming, believable and convincing, and their quiet, unobtrusive way makes them well liked. They win their clients over with their persistence.

If presenting in a sales role, they're not that good at the 'one-call' close. However, once they have won the client over, their ability to secure the relationship carries them through.

They love to work out of a 'step-by-step' process, appreciate structure and value what's been tried and is true, so will not come up with many new and innovative ideas. They err on the secure and safe side rather than taking any risks or promoting the latest fads.

When presenting to a Peaceful, like the Playful, they prefer you to build a rapport with them first. Share some common interest — they are willing listeners. They are fiercely loyal, so it's very difficult to dislodge existing relationships they've developed with others.

They will not choose to challenge, criticise or object to what you have to offer, and can appear to be most accommodating. They find it hard to say they are not interested in something, because they don't like conflict, so they may allow you to think that they are. Sometimes this can baffle the presenter.

They would never consider coming on strong, but have hidden strength, and don't like pushy people, especially those trying to sell them a product or idea. A key factor is to let them sleep on their decision.

Always offer to contact them, rather than the other way around — they prefer it that way.

Emails

The following is an example of how a Peaceful would send an email invitation to a meeting:

Dear Jennie,

Lately I have been thinking about your son Jeremy. Did he enjoy his time with VSA? What an experience for him. In our last conversation you said he was having a stopover in the islands before he got home. I look forward to hearing more from you about his adventure. I am also looking forward to catching up with you next week at our monthly meeting.

We will be focusing on the next phase of the project at this meeting, and I am keen to hear how everyone might be able to support this, and perhaps talk about some strategies that will help us. After speaking with the executive team it makes sense to work on this now.

Thanks for listening to Jacqui's concerns. She told me you were awesome when things fell apart.

I'll probably see you before this meeting, and I'll look forward to that.

Cheers

Susan

Relating socially

While these types won't necessarily organise a social event, they really enjoy attending them. They will come in and sit down, then watch the comings and goings of everyone else. Peacefuls are warm and inviting, and there is such an ease about them that people are attracted to them, especially in a business setting. They will set up their drinks and nibbles around them, happy for people to come to them, rather than taking the initiative themselves.

Some prefer to arrive late to social engagements, so they can hide in the crowd and guarantee that the person they click with most will already be there, or they will arrive as the event is just about to start, so they don't have to initiate conversation.

One thing that you need to be aware of about Peacefuls is their willingness to clean up and assist in any of the tasks required at a social function. They are our quiet servers, who need to be appreciated and valued — and often this gets overlooked.

Key drivers

Peacefuls are very reliable and loyal. At work, you can count on them to get things finished. They are excellent mediators, never taking sides — for their own preservation, too!

They dodge the bullets that can be fired on any business day. If there is a war going on in the workplace, they will pull away from the tension, because of their strong need for peace and harmony. (You never see them attaching themselves to other people's negative issues.) Once the war is won, they'll join the winning team! They are good at keeping their heads down and operating under the radar.

They are sensitive to others; they know when people are upset and can comfortably reach out. Peacefuls are wonderful listeners, which is why they are attracted to counselling, mediation and conciliation-type careers. They also have excellent administration skills. Tolerance, patience, the ability to process and finish well and being supportive are their strengths.

They are excellent at dampening down tempers. They know all the gossip and secrets in the workplace, because people feel an ease about sharing with them, but you could never pry it out of a Peaceful. They are fiercely loyal, salt of the earth types.

Peacefuls are very important to our world. Without them we would have communities and organisations that were constantly at war with one another. *Value them, give them respect* and just stand back and watch how they bring a positive aspect to those around them.

8 The Powerful personality

Words describing the Powerful

Highlight those words that describe you.

Adventurous	Authoritative	Brave
Change agent	Commanding	Competitive
Decision-maker	Daring	Doer
Enjoys challenges	Focused	Goal-driven
Independent	Impulsive	Likes to lead
Opinionated	Productive	Quick
Single-minded	Restless	Visionary

Because we can have characteristics from other personalities as well, these words may not exactly describe you, but if you are predominantly a Powerful you will recognise many of them and there will be a lot of things in this chapter that you will be able to identify with. If you work with — or probably under — a Powerful, this chapter will help you understand what motivates them.

Strengths

Powerfuls are strong visionaries, focusing on the future. They're big-picture types who see a world of possibilities, and go for them.

In terms of achieving, there is no one quite like the Powerful.

They are 'doers'. Highly driven, they are ambitious, goal-focused and decisive. They move quickly and exist to bring change, with a natural instinct to physically demonstrate and produce. They deliver consistently on words and actions, and therefore have an inborn ability to lead.

'Doing' is excitement and oxygen to them. They thrive in emergency situations, where they can see what needs to be done. They want to see immediate gains and their timeframe is *now*!

This raises the issue again of whether leadership is genetically infused (nature) or learned (nurture). I would say it's both, particularly for the Powerful. Of course, the challenge for Powerfuls is to lead in a positive way for the benefit of all. They love to take charge of anything that could bring them credit. Taking control, giving directions and correcting others come as naturally as breathing for them.

They can accomplish more in any given day than most, and in half the time. Being visionary types, they often have ten irons in the fire, yet are able to give equal time and attention to each of the goals and tasks that need to be accomplished. This is how they thrive.

Powerfuls appreciate honesty and candour, but this can get them into trouble. They are circumstantial, so what they think, they say. 'Don't take it personally,' they might say. 'We're here to do a job.' They can't help it: the blood in their veins carries their drive for change and results.

They flourish on opposition, and respect those who are willing to face challenges and respond by achieving outcomes.

Weaknesses

Powerfuls' endless abilities default to weaknesses when pushed to extremes. Because Powerfuls can see how to action things quicker than others, they want to seize the moment, and so may come across as bossy, impatient, domineering and insensitive. The judge, jury and executioner all wrapped in one person — that's the Powerful.

They prefer to do things themselves, so they get the credit. In defence, they would retort, 'No, I am not consciously wanting to be a Lone Ranger but, believe me, it's easier to do it myself, then I know the job will get done correctly and on time!'

Often they can take things on by default, because of what they see as the incompetence of others. They often get frustrated by the length of time others take to make decisions, get moving and achieve. They don't suffer fools, so the Powerful can do a pretty good job at trying to get rid of those 'incompetents' from the team. It's not like a baseball game: three strikes and you're out. You get one strike, and one strike only.

Powerfuls can come across as demanding and tyrannical when things aren't going at the pace they want, which can result in an autocratic working environment. Their restlessness can also turn the energy in the workplace into tension if things aren't moving quickly enough.

Because Powerfuls get the picture quickly, they are restless to the point that most meetings bore them, especially when they aren't at the helm. You can see them switch off and drift into other thoughts and plans as other types talk, look at the down-sides and go off on tangents. They don't really care if you don't like them. Its about productivity.

These Powerful bumper stickers say it all.

- 'Do not start with me, you will not win'
- 'If you aren't outraged, you're not paying attention'
- 'I don't get ulcers, I give 'em'
- 'I don't get mad, I get even'.

In the training room, I once asked a group Powerfuls how they thought they came across when operating out of their weaknesses. Proudly, they retorted:

- bossy, abrupt, frank, pushy
- control freak, short, cold, distant, arrogant, demanding, insensitive
- they can push too hard, when they feel there is incompetence

- careless of others' feelings, overpowering
- impatient, bitchy and aggressive
- too quick to decide and judge
- don't listen well, and
- impatient.

Visual clues
Clothing

The Powerful is a serviceable and practical dresser whose appearance is likely to impress (in a powerful way!). However, they can spend little attention or time on this issue.

For females, no high, kick-ass shoes for these types! They want to get to their destination in the shortest possible time, so their clothing has to assist them in this, not hold them back. You won't often see a Powerful female wear flowery or patterned outfits, as these would not reflect the Powerful personality.

Unsurprisingly, power-dressing is their preferred style: top-shelf, quality clothes have great appeal. Their hair style also needs to be practical and easy to maintain.

You wouldn't see them meandering around in shopping malls. Powerfuls shop with a focus and mission, to get what they need and then get out of there. For this reason internet shopping appeals, so they can get on and do other, much more important things.

Gestures and body language

These types are easy to spot. No written test is needed to find out who is a Powerful!

Powerfuls work at top speed — or overdrive! They move the fastest of the four personalities, with short, sharp gestures. They are keen to get their message across. A preferred stance is hands on hips, which can show in a non-verbal way that they have a strong presence, and can be intimidating. A dead giveaway is their index finger making holes in the air as they point or wag it inches away from someone's face.

Powerfuls do have a persuasive presence about them, but because they are determined, they can come across as intense and dominating in manner.

Because they move quickly, with focus, they can appear angry or tense. This is often misinterpreted by other personalities, which can cause all sorts of issues in the workplace. While they can come across as looking impatient, really it's because they have a myriad of things going on in their head that they are trying to work through.

You can see these types continually pushing the button at an intersection to try to hurry up the pedestrian phase. They don't have the luxury of time to just wait. These also are the types who have to move from lane to lane on the motorway, in the hope of getting to their destination quickly. They can't help themselves. Time is money. When standing at the doorway of opportunity, they don't ask themselves if they should go on in; they just stride on in and take control of the situation. They have a restlessness about them, and can pace as they talk.

When sitting (not their favourite stance) they have a tendency to tap their toes or rock their legs back and forth. Another annoying habit is clicking their pens. With high energy, they're desperate to move on to action.

When conversing, they don't mind invading your private space with direct eye contact. It's not long before you find yourself wedged up against the wall as they spout forth with passion about a business challenge or new idea.

Voice and tone
Powerfuls have a commanding and authoritative voice. Their speech is rapid, showing little emotion, but with clarity and forcefulness.

They are factual but not overly detailed, producing a 'Reader's Digest' condensed version. They hate long sentences and convoluted expressions, and prefer to be short and to the point. Powerfuls will tolerate a minor degree of small talk, as long as you pull everything together in a mini-summary at the end.

It's not their preference to be involved in idle chatter. They can come across as abrupt and cut right through your conversation if it is of no interest to them. Sometimes they are astounded that people feel intimated by them.

They love to talk about efficiency and organisation. If you can talk to them around these topics, you will have them engaged for as long as it takes.

Environment

The Powerful's environment doesn't have to be pristine and neat. They can work with files everywhere and in a bit of a mess, but just ask them to locate something and they will have it in front of them lickety-split. They want a serviceable environment that's not difficult to work in.

They love to display trophies and awards, so don't be surprised to see some recognition for their achievements hanging in their office: perhaps a framed certificate for a hole in one in golf, or a picture of them catching a blue marlin, or a snapshot of them with some high-profile high achiever.

Stress

Powerfuls default to working harder when under stress. They face their issues head on, so working harder may seem to them to be a solution. This makes them the personality type most prone to workaholism. They get their sense of value out of what they do, so 'doing' is the solution as far as they are concerned. Another stress-buster is to do something physical. Going for a run or a workout at the gym is good for them. Their natural endorphins kick in and they recover very quickly.

Often the poor person who is causing the stress will become the target, and look out: the Powerful may then go on a mission to get rid of them. Once the Powerful has had a thought like this, it's really history for the one targeted. The Powerful will plan and scheme all manner of ways to get rid of them.

You know when a Powerful is upset: they blow up, and other people tend to duck for cover.

It has been suggested that both Playfuls and Powerfuls find it easiest to express themselves through outbursts of anger, so they are more prone to high blood pressure which can cause heart attacks and other medical conditions.

Work

Powerfuls love the thrill of the chase, and are strongly competitive. Their timeframe is now, so when they say they will do something, it will be actioned immediately. They can have a tendency to push too hard, however, which can make other personalities dig in and resist the Powerful's orders. Also, their impatience with listening before acting can be a down-side.

Planning

The Powerful have a tendency to 'wing it' and under-plan. They achieve things, and fortunately have the ability to deliver the goods without having to spend endless hours in the planning stage. They just work it out as they go.

Leadership

The Powerful is a visionary leader. They have a natural feel for being in charge, and are very confident in their ability to achieve.

A friend and colleague from the airline industry told me about a Powerful who would, when you entered his office, either make you stand for a length of time before telling you to sit down, or virtually ignore you until he was ready to acknowledge your presence or listen to your questions. This was his way of letting his staff know he was the person in charge.

This kind of behaviour can quite often end up having a detrimental effect on a team, as it doesn't encourage the other Powerfuls within the group to grow. This management style is restrictive, as staff are not as free with their ideas and do not want to be put in an uncomfortable position when approaching a Powerful either for advice or to discuss an idea.

However, on the positive side, my friend also told me about a newly appointed company manager who announced that he was targeting a profit several times higher then the current goal. This was met with sceptical looks from his team, but they were all proven wrong when these new targets were not only met but exceeded.

If the Powerful's vision and drive wasn't as single-minded and strong, these results would not have been achieved. The Powerful quite often doesn't even contemplate failure as an option and always thrives on challenge.

Because they are so outcome-driven, Powerfuls can often be blinkered in the pursuit of achieving their goals.

Meetings

These types are happy to drive any meeting. In fact, they edge their way into the driver's seat pretty smartly. They keep meetings short and to the point. If someone goes off on a tangent the Powerful will either bring the meeting back into alignment or tell the person who is off track point-blank to sort themselves out. Powerfuls are happy to sort out anyone who is not co-operating.

If bored, they will go off in their mind planning something totally different to what is being discussed. This will be evident by the glazed look in their eyes.

Here is another example from my friend in the airline industry.

Having been involved in airline senior management for over 18 years, watching numerous changes of personnel over that time, the dynamics and personality types within the group make an interesting case study on Powerful personality types. Over the years we have had various people in charge of different divisions within the company, and generally there are always clear personality types related to the different divisions.

Most divisional managers tend to have an element of the Powerful in their personalities. To be head of their division they need to have a certain amount of drive and people skills, as every position around the table involves managing numerous staff. It is always interesting to watch the moulding of the new members to the group, particularly those with strong Powerful traits. They are often the ones who stride into the meeting and sit down close to the company manager. They are always organised with their action items and have minutes from previous meetings to give the impression that they are thoroughly on top of what they have undertaken.

In top-level meetings, where you have a number of Powerful personality types in the room, often everybody will use past stories as examples to back up issues they want to pursue. An obvious trait of the Powerfuls, who like to stamp their mark and prove their authority on issues, is to say what they have done. This is a behaviour Powerfuls are very comfortable with.

As you can probably gather, there is a certain amount of ego which goes hand in hand with the Powerful, and I always find it interesting to study the dynamics in various board and management groups. It is especially revealing to note the differences between genders. Women who have achieved at this level always appear to be more assertive and calculating than their male counterparts. I think this is predominantly due to the harder struggle which women tend to have to reach the higher levels of management. This is not a negative reflection on successful women in businesses; purely an observation based on a number of years of dealing with various management teams in New Zealand.

Managers in charge of executive groups quite often display extreme Powerful tendencies; some more of a joking nature and others to stamp their authority. An example of this is managers putting up their hand and saying 'Shush' as you would do to a young child. This is not necessarily appropriate for other senior managers, but due to the overt nature of the action it tends to get treated light-heartedly.

This is opposed to situations in which I have seen the person in charge of a group order food for himself in a meeting which has lasted through an evening break, and then sit there and eat while continuing the meeting. This is really stamping his authority, saying, 'You have to wait for your dinner.'

Decision-making

The Powerful are the best of all the personality types at making decisions. They are decisive and opinionated, and efficiency is key in their decision-making. If you want a quick decision, a Powerful will come up with the goods.

They have gut reactions and go with them. Even if they are later proved to be wrong, they know they will be able to recover somehow.

As a leader they will give others the freedom to make decisions, but it is loaded with the underlying threat of 'You'd better make the right one!'

Presenting

Powerfuls love the opportunity to present, enjoying the challenge and the power and prestige that it can bring. Their commanding presence means they come across as believable.

They can think on their feet quickly and respond accordingly, and are especially good on topics such as the bottom line, increasing efficiency, saving time, return on investments, and improving profits and productivity. Because they are change agents, they can offer several solutions to one issue.

When being presented to, Powerfuls can intimidate the presenter by asking for their credentials and how they are qualified to speak on the subject at hand. They would very rarely check these out; it's just their way of clearly letting you know they have the upper hand.

They are not interested in all the detail; they want to know about results, bottom lines and outcomes.

Powerfuls have a tendency to take the lead and quickly tell whomever is presenting how the meeting ought to and will be structured. They are comfortable with challenging a speaker, and can demand immediate responses to their questions. Their first question is likely to be 'How will this profit me?' or 'How will it benefit me?'. It's wise to give a Powerful supporting evidence of the answers to these questions.

Do not get caught up in idle chit-chat, or be vague and wishy-washy. Just get to the point. Always keep your presentation short and to the point — Powerfuls will appreciate it. Make it clear to the Powerful that you will take care of the details and are confident there will be a positive outcome.

Don't be afraid to make the 'close' — a Powerful respects that ability in others.

Emails

The following is an example of how a Powerful would send an email invitation to a meeting:

> Jennie
> Meeting Reminder
> 4.30 p.m. 3rd November
> Boardroom
> Refer to agenda sent on 28/10
> Good things ahead!
> Jon

Relating socially

When it comes to social engagements, it's not uncommon for Powerfuls to bring up business or sports in conversation. Remember they are outcome- and results-focused, therefore are most comfortable talking around something they feel is worthwhile. They find idle chit-chat a bore.

They are single-minded in their approach, so it's not unusual for them to initiate conversation with someone who they feel can offer them something. They get bored quickly, and are not afraid to say so or show it by cutting you off or ignoring you. Some people can feel intimidated by their confidence.

Powerfuls can be selective in their choice of social engagements to attend (unless, of course their spouse or partner has insisted they support them at something). You probably won't see them stay until the end of the night, either. They like to dictate what they are doing, and not having others try to do that.

They like to be *doing* something. Give them the barbecue tongs or something they can take charge of.

Key drivers

The Powerful's ability to take control and work to fulfill a vision and goal is always evident. These task-oriented, decisive types keep meetings moving onward and upward. They are hugely visionary, and can see things that others do not see.

Sleep interrupts their work. They thrive in a work environment; in fact, their greatest fear is the loss of their job or sickness, because if they can't work, they can't produce.

They won't bite your head off when you first meet them, but it won't take them long to find something wrong with your delivery and correct you on facts or figures, or challenge your credibility.

They are also cautious about putting themselves in a place where they can't win. If they can't play golf well, they will make other plans for places to do business.

Powerfuls have an ability to weasel out of situations that are not working in their favour, and sometimes seem to have more tricks than a monkey up their sleeve. They are also pretty good at stealing other people's ideas. They are not 'fence sitters'. They work hard and play hard.

Our Powerfuls definitely show their worth as they forge ahead, progressing and developing our economy. We need them on our team. They can be disruptive, but how else do we bring about change?

Give the Powerful *credit* and *appreciation* and you will find they will rise to any occasion and bring you with them.

9 Pressing the right buttons

Treat people as if they were what they ought to be and you help them to become what they are capable of being.
— *GOETHE*

You might now be saying, 'Now I have myself sussed — I know who I am, and my strengths and capabilities — how can I better relate to others by using this information?' If the FBI use it to get into the criminal mind, then surely we can use this same tool for the betterment of relationships and business. The magic of understanding personalities can turn any situation around if we only know how to respond to others from where they sit.

The Biblical saying, 'Do to others as you would have them do to you' only works in the playground, and in terms of manners, thoughtfulness and general courtesies. A better guideline is not 'Treat others the way *you* want to be treated', but 'Treat them how *they* want you to treat them.' Let's find out how that works in practice . . .

Playful
The greatest need a Playful has is for **attention, affection, approval** and **acceptance**.

These people won't make it difficult for you to give them that. Honestly, try it — it will work wonders.

Now you might say, 'Wouldn't everyone want this?' Yes, but not as much as the Playful. Every waking moment, every one of their actions is driven by this need. It's right up there with breathing, eating and sleeping! As Playfuls mature, they may not seek it so much from others, but be sure that this is their underlying, instinctive motivation and key driver.

In the airport example at the start of this book, the Playfuls were the ones who found the bar and made it a watering hole of people, refreshing themselves and others. Nothing could be more enjoyable for them — they stay buoyant when they are in the company of others.

They love fun environments, the exchanging of great stories, relationship building, recognition and especially acceptance and approval. Playfuls are easily pleased if you weave these four needs creatively into conversation and actions. You can play a big part in helping them to be more balanced if you relate to them from this premise.

How does this work in the workplace? Well, it's certainly not through criticism. The worst thing you can do is disapprove of a Playful. Criticise them and they will wilt like a flower.

The opposite to criticism is heaps of praise, acceptance and affirmation. Now that's more like it! Give them encouragement and there is no stopping them. They will respond by trying to please you and make your day. They will feel you are with them, supporting them, approving of them and cheering them on.

You might be thinking, 'Praise, acceptance, affirmation . . . what kind of ego am I developing in these types by doing this?' Well, if you don't give it to them, they will just go somewhere else where they can get it — they're wired that way.

No one wakes up one morning and says 'I'm off to have an affair!' No, these situations arise because someone's tank is empty. The Playful is especially sensitive to these needs. Give them what they need — at home and at work — so they don't go wandering.

Show a bit of warmth, openness and approval towards them, and you will have a committed, wonderful, willing worker, one who brings energy, creativity, new ideas and fun to the workplace. This is what motivates them.

Powerful

Their greatest needs are **credit for all that they do and achieve**, **appreciation**, and **to be shown loyalty**.

It doesn't take a rocket scientist to realise that sitting around at an airport would not be their favourite pastime. They love to fill their day with activity, and would see this as hugely unproductive time. An airport disruption would make them feel as if they were being kept in a holding cell — yes, even a well-appointed private members' lounge would be considered that by these types — unless there was someone or something there that could add to their purposes or plan.

As an aside, most Powerfuls do not like flying. Allowing other people, even pilots, to be in command and in control of their destiny is difficult for them. Interestingly, I have heard many high-profile businessmen express their distaste for flying. Often this was evident without them even admitting to it, but I could tell through observing the expressions on their faces and their body language; seeing them pacing back and forth, the palms of their hands all clammy, and beads of sweat on their upper lips as they approach the airbridge to board an aircraft. This is, of course, because they like to feel their feet solidly on the ground, and that they're in control of the task at hand. That is what gets their juices going.

For the Powerful, being appreciated for all they accomplish gives them even more energy and drive. They soften and are easier to relate to when others make a conscious effort to meet this need. In fact, you may even get them to listen to you! So when their fists smash down on the service desk, demanding to know, 'When is the fog going to lift?', you need to empathise with where they are coming from before you can get some connection and rapport. By understanding that they want things done *now*, you can appreciate that the sooner they can get out of the airport the better.

Powerfuls don't suffer fools, so be sure to speak in the short and to-the-point style they favour. Do not waft words about or hesitate.

Commiserate with lines like, 'I can imagine that you have important meetings to chair, that possibly depend heavily on your contribution' or 'I can't get you to your destination right now, but what I can do is arrange a conference call so you can take control of those meetings you have planned'. Oohhh, their knees give way with a response like that. They are intoxicated by such statements. You can virtually see their emotional tank being filled as you speak. 'Finally, someone understands me,' they say under their breath.

They may even want to take you home! One day a businessman in the lounge handed me his business card on departure, and said 'I don't know how you do this, but I always leave this lounge feeling better than when I came in. When you tire of your husband, please give me a call. I go home to a wife who rarely encourages me, and stands at the front gate with an imaginary bucket of ice water, ready to throw it over all my new ideas, dreams and goals.'

Trust me, Powerfuls *need* appreciation and recognition. Give 'em plenty, or they may go looking for it elsewhere.

Usually it's natural for the Powerful to climb the ladder of success quickly. They have tons of ability, not because they are necessarily smarter, but they are astute and constantly have their antenna up, scanning for ideas and opportunities and then acting on them, thus getting the accolades they deserve.

Give them responsibility — something to get their teeth into. Be decisive and talk about results, efficiency and organisation and they'll respond.

Precise

Precise types need *sensitivity, space, silence* and *support*.

Coming back to the airport lounge scenario, because their sharp minds are extremely organised and they are 'time smart', the Precise would use their critical skills to utilise this inconvenience effectively, especially if they have the tools to work with. They are always well prepared, so would have a Plan B on hand, and would expect you to have some options to offer them.

Being sensitive enough to read these people's needs is a vital ingredient to making them feel valued. For instance, personally inviting them into the business centre so they can work in a quiet environment really makes them feel that you are honouring them in the best possible way.

When a Precise approaches me, those four 's' words are uppermost in my mind as I look for ways to best communicate with them. They want you to be sensitive to their needs, to be insightful and intuitive about their world, acknowledging their circumstances and the inconvenience. They would like you to be thoughtful about and considerate of how they see this situation and, most importantly, to support them as much as you can. Thoughtful gestures go down big time with a Precise.

They operate best where it's quiet, and can feel overwhelmed by crowds, noise and clutter. Their brain doesn't operate to its fullest potential if they have to work in that kind of environment. Give them an office to themselves, with a door, or a place where it's private and quiet, and you will be astonished by how much work they can plough through. *Space* and *silence* are the key words here.

Whether you are the boss or colleague of a Precise, supporting them in what they are doing will ignite in them a strong desire to back you all the way. If you don't, just watch these ones withhold information pertinent to the task. They have their special way of controlling others and letting things crumble around them.

Peaceful

The Peaceful's needs are **respect, value, loyalty** and **harmony**.

When I worked at the airport, I received the greatest number of unsolicited letters of thanks for the way they were looked after from Peacefuls. Acknowledging their patience and kindness as they waited out the fog would put me on the right foot with them immediately.

Often Peacefuls get overlooked, as they aren't known to make demands, and can therefore be perceived as content. They can feel upset, but tend to internalise it rather than make a disappointed comment. If they feel overlooked and ignored they remember this, and won't come back.

These low-key types don't ask for much in life, but you can truly connect with them if you give them what they need. They have been wired with a need to be valued for who they are, not necessarily what they do. Recognising how they add to any environment and, just as importantly, acknowledging their attributes — patience, loyalty, faithfulness, stability, commitment, consistency, trustworthiness, dependability, interest in others — can have a huge impact on the Peaceful. Respecting them for their ability to not cause conflict would have them instantly move towards both you and the task in their workplace.

You also need to understand that Peacefuls do need some time to relax — they get their energy and motivation from that. It's their 'top up'. Taking regular breaks spurs them on, and they will finish a task well if these are provided.

Above all, when change is imminent, make sure you prepare them for it, and give them reasons why it is occurring. Don't make changes for the sake of it. Give them time to reflect and work through the rationale.

As Peacefuls are the hardest to motivate, externals don't affect them, you need to consider how best to connect with them. If you don't genuinely affirm their attributes, you will discover how hard it can be to get them going.

Make sure you monitor the amount of responsibility you give them. They are capable of taking things on, but make sure they want to.

Personality type	Basic desire	Key needs and motivations
Playful	To have fun	Attention — loves an audience Affection Approval Acceptance of who they are
Powerful	To have control	Credit for their abilities and accomplishments

Personality type	Basic desire	Key needs and motivations
		Appreciation for all they have done — recognition and results
		Loyalty in the ranks — loves to lead
		New challenges
Precise	To get it right	Sensitivity to their feelings
		Space to be alone — 'don't crowd me!'
		Silence
		Support when down or from peers — 'I believe in you'
Peaceful	To have peace	Feeling respected
		Being valued for who they are, not what they do
		Lack of stress
		Peace and quiet
		Time and encouragement

Remember:

Playfuls are instinctively spontaneous, energised and creative. They like to have choices. They hate being tied down to just one option.

Powerfuls are instinctively decisive and want results right away. They have a preference for being in control.

Precise types are instinctively particular and deliberate. They just can't relax if everyone's not putting all their effort into projects, tasks and activities. They are very rational and objective, and prefer you to communicate that way when dealing with them.

Peacefuls are instinctively considerate, good listeners, and prefer it if you are caring, inclusive and non-confrontational.

Personality pairings

— how the different types can
relate to each other

You'll never know till you try to reach them how accessible people are,
but you must approach each person by the right door.
— *Henry Ward Beecher,* Proverb from a Plymouth Pulpit, *1887*

Operating out of our natural strengths and abilities has greater
magnitude when we are working with others. However, there are
times when it is necessary to work out of behaviours and traits that
are not our norm and can seem so foreign to us. I find this especially
helpful when meeting new people and establishing some mutual
ground.

Of course, this is a fine line. If you try to modify your personality
too much it can be counterproductive, draining you of energy and
causing people to view you with distrust and caution. I am not
advocating sacrificing your own authenticity, but it can be helpful to
occasionally check to see if you are too extreme in your behaviours,
which could cause others to react badly to you or shut down. This
is not losing yourself but genuinely trying to get along and connect
with others.

I wouldn't advise you to spend too much time working from a
different perspective, as it would exhaust you, but give enough to
the other person so that some rapport is built.

Imagine drawing a circle around the words in the centre of the
personality profile quadrant (see page 26), and aim to operate from
there, so you can relate to all personalities. If you are too extreme

in any one area, there is no way that you will be able to successfully relate to the other personalities, but by tempering those extremes, you will draw people to you and experience fewer 'personality clashes'. To make an impact and influence others, you need to reach beyond yourself, and reveal their potential and possibilities.

The mark of a great leader and influencer is having the ability to bring out the latent gifts and abilities in others. Understanding personalities helps us identify them, and also helps us to adapt in order to relate better to others.

For example, being a Playful myself, I quickly realised that in my manager's role at the airport, if I was going to be an effective leader I needed to modify some of the things I did that could agitate other personalities.

I love to talk. Can you see how this would get the Precises' backs up? They want less talk and more action. From where they sit, they could see this 'chit chat' as not being focused or attempting to accomplish the task. Therefore it wouldn't be long before they would start feeling frustrated.

A Powerful would find my talking tedious as well, considering my conversation far too flippant and unproductive for them. I would come across as unprofessional. It's happened, believe me!

Talking the language of the hearer creates far better communication between two people. The secret is finding some mutual ground, or area of cohesion. If we are to forge good working relationships with others, we need to think about ways to do this. Knowing what to look for and meeting the needs of others goes a long way to improving relations in the workplace. We all know deep down that others will connect and engage with us once they know we are interested and care about them. So, let's look at the different combinations that arise . . .

Playful
Playful relating to Powerful
The common thread between these two personalities is an outgoing, unrestrained, extroverted manner. Both love to initiate dialogue

— although with different motivations. For Powerfuls, dialogue is about getting results and achieving. For Playfuls, dialogue is for building relationships. Powerfuls don't really enjoy small talk and this is what Playfuls feel most comfortable with.

Because Playfuls love to connect, it's not uncommon for them to hug or touch on meeting. Powerfuls don't, so respect that about them. Playfuls need to minimise their hand gestures and impulsiveness, so the Powerful is not distracted by them.

Powerfuls, with every fibre of their being, are task-oriented, while Playfuls will do the task only if they have a relationship with those they are working with, and preferably if it's fun.

So when working with a Powerful, the Playful needs to consider ways to add value to what the Powerful would like to achieve. Playfuls have such a need to be accepted that they will go all out to be co-operative, obliging and supportive to assist the Powerful's vision.

They have a healthy respect for the Powerfuls, as they say what they think, whether it hurts or not. This can really throw the Playfuls, however. Powerfuls can bring them down by addressing their unnecessary frivolity or the many tangents they may go off on. Powerfuls would prefer Playful types to work in a more formal and businesslike manner, sticking to the agenda and goal. Being mindful of this aids in building some synergy with them.

Like the Precise, Powerfuls prefer you talk to them about what you think, rather than what you feel, which comes naturally for the Playful. They are more objective than subjective, and won't stay in conversations too long when people are talking on a feelings basis. They would prefer you to be thinking about outcomes and results.

While Powerfuls plan by the seat of their pants, they still plan, and expect others to do the same. Overselling your abilities will not cut it with the Powerfuls, and they will not shy away from challenging you.

Powerfuls speak more directly and to the point than Playfuls, so mirroring that in conversation will definitely help in any meeting or workplace. Playfuls should lessen their demonstrative expressions. not go off on tangents, and keep to the point.

Playful relating to Precise

A lot of energy is created by the Playfuls, so Precise types try to avoid them. They don't see things from the same perspective: one is noisy, one is quiet. The Playfuls are outgoing and have a strong need to be with people; the Precise are very private and self-sufficient and can happily work alone. They're as different as chalk and cheese!

Because Playfuls are an open book, they invariably find it a challenge to draw out any personal detail from Precise types. The more open Playfuls are, the more closed the Precise become.

They will give you detail all right, but not on the human element. Rather, it will be detail on how the project is going, a list on who arrived late to work, or possibly substantial evidence on forecasting the next phase of the project. Facts, facts and more facts. They are a huge source of information. However, this doesn't work for a Playful unless the Precise has first shown interest in them as a person.

Playfuls, try putting some practicalities and detail into your conversation and see how the Precise move towards you. Yes, it's foreign to you, but collaborative teams have to put in some effort!

Playfuls also need to lessen their need to tell all. Perhaps approach the Precise in a more methodical way. They would appreciate you bringing an agenda or checklist of what you need to do together, and working through this with no deterrents and interruptions.

Remember to use your social graces and manners. Always turn your cellphone off when dealing with them, and never — I mean *never* — answer it if you have inadvertently left it on. This would be remembered forever, and held against you.

The Precise's preference is to approach the task at hand and complete it. The Playful will abandon the task in preference of the relationships at hand. That would not be a high priority for the Precise; they don't even think that way.

Because Playfuls are at ease talking on a feelings level, they need to remember the Precise aren't. They are more comfortable speaking around facts and logic. If you can produce facts in the early part of a meeting with these types, they will definitely move toward you.

Because Playfuls are noisy in many instances, it is wise if they lower their voice and don't dominate the conversation when dealing with a Precise. Don't be afraid of silences — a Precise is comfortable in them. The Playful can feel very uncomfortable, however. They need to remind themselves that these silences are not directed personally at them. It's about the Precise trying to restore their soul in the quietness. To dig deep and reflect on the day is imperative for them.

I saw an example of this recently. After a day's training, a Precise business colleague felt exhausted and drained by having been around people all day. When we arrived at the airport, he quietly removed himself from the group, and even politely refused an invitation into the Frequent Flyers lounge. He had 'had it' with people for the day.

We looked down from the mezzanine and there he was on his own, reading a book. The Playfuls in the group wanted to go and 'rescue' him and bring him up to the party, but giving thought to their new-found information about different personalities, they realised he was OK.

If you are married to one, you know jolly well that you can travel from one city to another with no conversation. The Precise person will be extremely happy, but usually the Playful is going nuts with frustration, as they long to talk!

What you are as a Playful, as a Precise, they're not, and what you're not, they are. It pretty much comes down to that. However, it is actually quite helpful that these two are extreme opposites, as it makes them easier to read than some other combinations that are more blurry or hazy.

> Key insight
> Playfuls need *attention, affection, approval* and *acceptance.*
> Precises need *space, sensitivity, silence and support.*

Playful relating to Peaceful

Both fiercely relational, it's easy for these two types to get on well. They both need a jolt, though, when it comes to staying on task and completing, especially when there is a deadline. Playfuls get sidetracked with interruptions that seem much more exciting, and Peacefuls are happy to just plod along at a speed comfortable to them.

The Peaceful are good at finishing tasks, but not at the speed a Playful would want. Time is not of the essence for Peacefuls. They know they will finish, but it will be at their own rate.

With this combination, neither one would want to address issues that are irritating them, as they hate any form of confrontation. They will avoid it at all costs. It's important also for the Playful to remember to not put the Peaceful on the spot, unprepared. This is an enormous stress for them, although you would never see it — it gets absorbed internally.

Playfuls are excitable communicators and talk fast, so they need to be considerate and slow down and sit in silence occasionally around the Peacefuls. Playfuls also have a tendency to butt in and interrupt (you can't help it, I know — you have so many stories that you feel you need to tell) but doing this will cause a Peaceful to shut up even more. Honouring the Peaceful's viewpoint will encourage them to speak up. By reflecting back the comments they make, you can draw these gentle ones into the conversation, resulting in them feeling valued.

Peacefuls are acutely aware how people push them and ride roughshod over them. Playfuls, without realising it, will try to draw Peacefuls into what they want to do. Peacefuls are an audience of willing listeners, so Playfuls love them and tend to seek them out. They are very accommodating, and will oblige you even more if you are accommodating to them in return, especially when the heat is on.

If you want to sing from the same page, Playfuls, value Peacefuls first as a person, listen to them, and gently draw them out.

Playful relating to another Playful

Of course, they understand each other well, but this combination can also be a challenge, as they both want to talk, both want to be the shining star, and neither is that great at listening. They both have more ideas than they could ever deliver on in a lifetime, neglecting the tasks that need to be done.

I remember driving into the city with another Playful business colleague. We were having the best conversation, both talking over each other and laughing. My colleague said, 'Allie, what did I just say?' I said, 'I don't know, I was too busy talking!' I then said, 'Andrew, what did I just say?' and he said, 'I don't know!'

Do you think it bothered us? Of course not! We just enjoyed the time together.

Its obvious that one of the Playfuls would have to do some adjusting if there was going to be an on-going, effective relationship. It will depend on how mature one of the two can be. In situations like this, the one who is happy to play second fiddle in the conversation or task shows themself to be the most mature. It won't be easy, but with effort and focus on the common good, it can be achieved. Going into a conversation with this in mind can really benefit the relationship.

Powerful

Powerful relating to Playful

Both personalities are high-energy types. Because the Powerful is more task-oriented and the Playful more relational, this can be the irritant when it comes to truly trying to relate.

Powerfuls can be impatient, and their 'cut to the chase' style can intimidate the Playful, which may pressure them to the point of them abandoning what is required. They can even start stuttering when they feel the Powerful's impatience with them.

Powerfuls' conversation is around organisation, outcomes and efficiencies. Playfuls' conversation is more around people and what's been happening lately, as well as ideas. They have a tendency to speak to hear their thoughts, which comes across to the Powerful as a lot of babbling rubbish, not worth listening to.

Start here, you Powerfuls. Listen. Be more open in your approach. Show some tolerance (hard, I know). Be aware of how you are perceived. Sometimes you aren't aware that you look as if you are mad at the world. You know it's more a matter of having so much on your mind, but others don't understand that.

Playfuls will warm to you if you ask about them as a person, and about what's going on in their lives. Disclosing a bit about yourself will make them feel more accepted and included by you. Feelings matter to the Playful, whereas Powerfuls have them right under control. Cut them some slack when it comes to working in a fun environment — you will see greater productivity if you do.

Now I know this would take great restraint for you Powerfuls, but believe me you will get great results if you give consideration to what the Playful appreciates. They will then be happy to do as you command! Think of it as getting more troops for your army.

Key insights

Powerfuls need *credit* and *appreciation*.

Playfuls need *attention, affection, approval* and *acceptance*.

Powerful relating to Precise

Each respects the other's ability to stay focused on what needs to be done. This is a good place to start when relating to each other. Other than that, these two personalities can be quite different.

Because the Powerful has a 'big picture', visionary approach, this is where these two can get unstuck. The Precise prefer to look back, use historical information and work out what was successful from that, then put a plan in place and work from there in a strategic way. Powerfuls are not that interested in data and detail.

How they perceive time is different, too. For Powerfuls, time is of the absolute essence. They have more to achieve and time is money. Precise types do not like unreasonable deadlines, and Powerfuls have a tendency to put these in place. Because Precises are so methodical, they will not be pushed to quicken their pace, so in order to work together it may be necessary for the Powerful to slow up and try to mirror the progress of the Precise.

Precise types are very private, while Powerfuls have a tendency to say what they think. This can cause a lot of non-verbal tension in meetings, as the Precises just watch and analyse, often expressing their disapproval in a silent way. This drives the Powerful nuts, as they can't totally read the Precise. A good place to start is to ask the Precise person how they would approach a certain task or project — and listen to them!

Also, if you manage to find their passion for a subject, hobby or interest, there is no stopping the Precise, and you won't be able to shut them up. The Powerful will find this really testing. They usually have to finally say, 'So what is your point?'

> ## Key insight
> Powerfuls need *credit* and *appreciation*.
> Precises need *sensitivity*, *space*, *silence* and *support*.

Powerful relating to Peaceful

There's not a lot of commonality here. Working in this combination would be the greatest challenge for either side. The Peacefuls would say that the Powerfuls just override and bulldoze and can treat them as less than human sometimes. I'm sure the Powerfuls would disagree!

Powerfuls, your body language can help tremendously here. When you speak, be affirming with your body language. Smile, and be more open. Don't be so intense and lessen your straight-up manner. If you don't, these intimidating mannerisms can cause Peacefuls to pull back. Sit down instead of standing over them, and try to relax.

A Powerful's directness can really throw a Peaceful, so try talking around issues rather than going straight to them. The best thing to do is talk less and listen more. Take a Peaceful out for a coffee. Buy two, one for you and one for them. Buy only one muffin, and shove it in your mouth so you can listen! It works.

I know this is frustrating for Powerfuls, as there can be a lot of pauses in the Peaceful's conversation, which is 'down-time' from the Powerful's point of view. But these listeners see more than most, and can read others well. Because they are people oriented, they prefer to have a conversation around them as a person before getting into the business side of things.

The Powerful has a strong business mindset, and it is frustrating for them when others don't experience it to the same degree. Remember that the Peaceful are brilliant at mediation, have a softening effect around tension and, because they listen so well, bring clarity to the table.

Most importantly, we must give these ones time: time to process, time to explore, time to reflect and time to express. Relax with them. It's worth the wait. If you do they will be your greatest allies and extremely loyal to the cause.

> **Key insight**
>
> Powerfuls need *credit* and *appreciation*.
>
> Peacefuls need *respect* and *to be valued*.

Powerful relating to another Powerful

Now this is an interesting combination. While they are both task-oriented, they both like to have an opinion, and this is where a bit of 'head to head' might occur. They are both wanting to take the helm, and this is probably their biggest threat to each other.

They respect each other's ability to achieve. However, the trade-off would be any form of meaningful relationship. It would be marred and challenged by competition. Powerfuls don't care if they're not liked: what's important are the results and achievement, so they focus on the task at hand.

Like the Playful–Playful pairing, a good place to start is by showing some maturity, with one person giving up their right to be the number one Head Honcho. That wouldn't hurt occasionally, would it? Just occasionally! It would only be your pride that you would have to grapple with.

Powerfuls prefer to work as Lone Rangers, so another challenge is seeking what others consider to be the best outcome. They avoid situations where they can't win, and will never put themselves up for something they aren't strong in. This win-at-all-costs mentality can help them win the war, but not have anyone following.

For others observing two Powerfuls, it can look as if they are in conflict with each other. They certainly both speak the same language. When working in this combination, both Powerfuls need to listen more, and soften their directness, which I am sure will do good things for the relationship.

> ## Key insight
> Both Powerfuls need *credit* and *appreciation*.

An example of two Powerfuls

My current manager is a very interesting mix of very strong Powerful combined with some Playful personality. When I approach my manager for some advice or want to talk to him about some issue, I always go to his office and close the door behind me, which is my way of saying, 'Hey, I need your attention.' I think it is my Powerful trait saying, 'I need your undivided attention', with no disrespect intended to my manager. He is usually so busy thinking about numerous issues it is not uncommon for him to be typing an email and saying quite clearly to me, 'Carry on, I'm listening.' On occasion he has answered the phone on his desk, followed by answering his mobile at the same time, all the while nodding at me and waving me on with his hand to carry on our conversation.

This is a classic case of a Powerful having too many irons in the fire at

the same time, and a case of physical actions struggling to keep up with
an over-active mind. If I didn't know this stuff, I know I would be more of
a reactor than a responder. I sit back and chuckle to myself about it more
these days.

Precise
Precise relating to Playful
For the Precise, this combination in a working relationship is the
one that needs the most effort. The Precises look at what needs to be
done, and the Playfuls are focused on the people who will eventually
do it. That in itself says enough. Understanding just this one point
will help you as you put some thought into how you can move
towards the Playful in the way they need.

Precise types find Playfuls frustrating in that they seem to display
a huge need for attention. Of course we all need to feel valued, and
yes, it's nice to feel others are making you feel that way, but the
Precise see the Playful as being totally OTT. They will do anything
for approval.

Playfuls love to play, and this is not high on a Precise's list — well,
not until the work is completed.

Precises need to think about how the Playfuls need to feel connected,
and try to give this to them, so the desired outcome can be achieved. If
they don't, the Playful will find it hard to stay on task or keep engaged.

Because the Precise are more formal, it helps if they can relax
more around Playfuls, giving them approval through eye contact
and, more importantly, smiling at them. Those non-verbal signals
create a more inviting front. Playfuls continually search for faces
that are giving an approving smile, and find the Precise most sparing
in giving them.

Does it really matter if the stapler isn't put back in its proper
place? Those things that the Precise have a need to put right, in the
greater scheme of things, do they really matter? When the Precise is
trying to build any sort of relationship with these fun-loving types,
these things can instantly kill it for them.

Praising a Playful for what they did do instead of constantly berating them for what they didn't can go a long way in effective relationship building. It's easy for the Precise to withhold praise and affirmation. Because of their high ideals, they think, 'The Playful never come through with the goods, so why should I praise them?' Sadly, the Playful wilts under this sort of treatment, and their productivity decreases as a result.

Precise people have a tendency to talk on a 'facts' level. Talk more on a 'feelings' level with Playfuls and you will have their support. Try it and see how differently they respond to you.

> ## Key insight
> Precises need *sensitivity, space, silence* and *support.*
>
> Playfuls need *attention, affection, approval* and *acceptance.*

Precise relating to Powerful

Their common thread is that they are both task-focused. The Powerful are more expressively sure of themselves than the Precise, who are more internally calculating. Precises can have a brilliant mind but they tend to talk themselves way beyond what they need to. When feeding back to a group, they expound on the highlighted points and can bore others with their response — especially the Powerful.

Because the Powerful has a natural tendency to speak up, delivering their opinion in a commanding way, the Precise can take their response as a slight, and can carry this for a long time.

The Precise doesn't act or move as quickly as the Powerful, which in itself can cause tension. Powerfuls are 'now!' types, while the Precise wouldn't consider making decisions without having thoroughly explored the ins and outs of an issue.

Their conversation styles also differ. Powerfuls speak very quickly and to the point. Precises prefer to bring their case with a huge amount of data. Precise types need to be prepared to go out of their comfort zone and step up the pace when dealing with Powerfuls. They need to make a decision and work out the scheme afterwards, giving less information than they think is required.

Powerfuls can be highly frustrated by the way Precise types hedge around discussions and don't say what they think. Just considering this will build bridges between these two types.

Powerfuls can perceive the Precise as wasting so much time on data, consequently blowing the budget on unnecessary preparation. Try working with two options rather than six.

Because the Precise are black and white, rules are security to them. A word of advice: don't accentuate rules with the Powerful, as they will turn off. Also, Precises love the written word, while the Powerful prefer the spoken word. Understanding where the other person is coming from will help you to relate better.

> Key insight
>
> Precises need *sensitivity, space, silence* and *support.*
>
> Powerfuls need *credit* and *appreciation.*

Precise relating to Peaceful

These two have a commonality in that they are not high-energy types, but are more low key. However, they are still quite different in the way they see things. Peacefuls are more relational and Precises more task-oriented. Peacefuls want harmony and security as their highest priority, so providing this can help them operate more efficiently.

As the Peaceful would rather listen, it is helpful for the Precise to think about asking open questions, and then to practise active listening. These people do not want to be known or treated as a human machine, but as a human being. This is important to them. Their role at work is secondary to who they are as an individual. This is a way you can affirm them.

Precises have a tendency to be private and self-reliant, so they need to temporarily connect with the Peacefuls in order to move forward. It helps to demonstrate some warmth and openness. Build some rapport by asking them about their family or something that is important to them.

They will not go for data as much as a Precise, but they do enjoy working on projects. Remember though — it will be at their pace, not yours.

With these two types working together, the atmosphere is likely to be low energy and quieter than the other combinations. Precise types prefer to work alone, but the Peaceful likes the company of others. Making an effort at break times to converse will bring some collaboration.

> ## Key insight
> Precises need *sensitivity, space, silence* and *support.*
>
> Peacefuls need *respect* and *to be valued.*

Precise relating to another Precise

Now this is where you might suffer paralysis by analysis syndrome! Both will have a huge love of accuracy and data, so this combination can easily get bogged down in the detail, as they keep adding to and refining it.

If two Precises have any form of disagreement, it can get blown way out of proportion. Like a stuck needle on a record, each one will want to prove they were right, revisiting the offence and wasting precious time trying to prove the point. This can impact on maintaining healthy relationships with those they are working with.

Because both Precises want to get the job done right, they can lean towards indecisiveness as they scrutinise every detail, checking and rechecking, bringing up the point again and again — not only to prove they are right, but to see if it could be done in a better way.

Someone in this combination will need to step outside their usual natural abilities to forge ahead. Let go of the need to be right. It achieves nothing. You may win the battle, but not the war!

> ## Key insight
> Both Precises need *sensitivity, space, silence* and *support.*

Peaceful

Peaceful relating to Playful

There is a strong commonality between these types, as they both love strengthening relationships. But this combination may come unstuck because both parties relate too much, spending too much time talking about family and friends, getting distracted and going off on tangents, and not achieving what needs to be done.

Playfuls have a tendency to do things in half the time a Peaceful would take, working, talking, thinking and walking faster than them. They are ideas people and are very creative. This is something Peacefuls find difficult. A Peaceful once said to me, 'I don't have an original thought in my head!'

As a Peaceful, if you have a Playful who is significant to your business or role, consider ways in which you can enhance the relationship by bending a bit or moving towards them. Because you are so relaxed, it can send a message that you are not enthusiastic. Start thinking about your body language. While you know you are considerate and thoughtful, the Playful would probably like to see you demonstrate this by engaging in a non-verbal way, such as leaning forward or sitting upright and looking interested.

The Peaceful taking the risk of speaking out more on issues will also help in this relationship. Playfuls are the most forgiving personality type, so they will respond with great empathy to seeing you try. Playfuls also love to be accepted, so they will take any crumb of attention that is thrown to them.

> ### Key insight
> Peacefuls need *respect* and *to be valued.*
> Playfuls need *attention, affection, approval* and *acceptance.*

Peaceful relating to Powerful

These two personalities have totally opposite thinking styles. The Powerful is decisive and action-oriented. They prefer to deal with issues head-on. Their focus is on setting goals and getting results, whereas the Peaceful is more relational. It's not that the Peaceful don't want results, it's more in the process that they differ.

In relating to a Powerful, the Peaceful needs to consider being more direct and decisive, maybe even going so far as setting some goals around the workplace. Of course this is not natural for the Peaceful, but necessary if there is going to be any relationship with a Powerful. It's not that they need to lose themselves and change who they are, just temporarily adjust for the sake of the initial contact.

The way the Peaceful can put off pressing issues or procrastinate can rankle with a Powerful. You Peacefuls know it's probably because you might have to deal with problems relating to an issue that has some tensions or conflict tagged on.

Peacefuls, try to occasionally initiate contact with these Powerfuls — they will respect you more. Perhaps getting up from your desk and going to the Powerful, rather than waiting for them to come to you, would help. Step up your pace. Make decisions today rather than sleeping on them. Stating facts, rather than what you think, will go a long way as well. It won't be easy, but Powerfuls are hugely decisive, and move towards those that share this quality.

If you have to work with a Powerful, think about how you can defuse some of their irritation because of your hesitation in voicing issues. Yes, it will be temporarily painful, but in the long run I guarantee it will work.

> ## Key insight
> Peacefuls need *respect* and *to be valued*.
> Powerfuls need *credit* and *appreciation*.

Peaceful relating to Precise
Neither are dynamic, 'out there' types, and so are happy to be out of the limelight. Precise types want more detail and structure than Peacefuls, and you can expect them to ask for it . They are more task-oriented so in relating to them, Peacefuls need to consider giving this some serious attention.

Because the Peaceful is relaxed, the Precise would appreciate them stepping up and being more decorous, especially around work issues. The Precise communicates in a facts and logic way, rather than subjectively — by that I mean they like conversation about what they think about a certain thing rather than how they feel about it.

They rarely want to relate on a personal level, or share their feelings soon after meeting you. This means they can be seen as distant and cool, but don't be offended by it. They are just private people who need lots of space. Being mindful of this as you converse will have a huge impact in the working relationship.

Because Precise types like to produce with excellence, by giving data, facts and practical strategies, they also expect this in return. Take time to think about how you can give them what they need, or at least bear this in mind.

> Key insight
>
> Peacefuls need *respect* and *to be valued.*
>
> Precises need *sensitivity, space, silence* and *support.*

Peaceful relating to another Peaceful

A pair of Peacefuls will be very comfortable in each other's company, but because they value relationships, it can prevent them from achieving outcomes. The desire for forming relationships can impact on their time management, goal achievement and results. Both would need to consider this and how they might use behaviours, traits and strengths that are more common to the other personalities to help the team move forward together.

Because Peacefuls would rather listen than talk, the energy and atmosphere where a pair of Peacefuls work could be quieter and more lifeless than that of other personalities. While this may appeal to the Peacefuls, it may not appeal to others working with them.

The Peacefuls could challenge each other to meet deadlines to keep things ticking over, although that would be something quite foreign to both of them!

Peacefuls are great administrators, and enjoy processing. Building in lots of small, incremental breaks to their day might infuse more energy and love for their work.

> ## Key insight
> Both Peacefuls need *respect* and *to be valued*.

Summary
When working in a team, you sometimes have to develop the skills of other personalities in order to achieve what needs to be done. Being aware of how others see a situation will give you a greater understanding of how to deal with those you are relating to.

It's so easy to say, 'This is just the way I am', and refuse to bend towards others. Well, go ahead, but you will find that the same people-issues will present themselves as you go through life.

All you have to do is show some consideration to those who look at life and work differently from you. Remember they are *different* — not wrong, just different!

I'd like to emphasise that you don't need to continuously operate out of a place that is not natural to you, but it is so useful when first getting into relationships with others, to build rapport and start working in a collaborative way.

Moving towards another personality helps us to sing from the same page. This can take great effort, but I can promise you it will help when working with others who look at the world differently. So often when we expect others to be just like ourselves, the result is frustration and tension. Moving toward an opposite, just for a moment, helps bridge the gap.

Pressing the wrong buttons

— how different personalities can create conflict and frustration

While we are considering how best to relate to others, we also need to look within ourselves and see how we might cause conflict and frustrate others by operating out of our own personalities. Remember, when pushed to extremes or out of balance your strengths become weaknesses. Weaknesses pushed to extremes become compulsions.

These are what we default to when under stress.

I am not suggesting that every type will always demonstrate these behaviours, but it is helpful to understand that aspects which begin as strengths, through circumstances, pressure and stress, can be easily expressed as weaknesses.

We all operate out of our natural traits, as these maintain our energy level and can keep us focused on our commitment to the task at hand. But with each personality type seeing circumstances and situations differently, this can cause frustrations when working with others.

View this as a warrant of fitness check on yourself, so you can avoid difficulties in the future! Being aware of the contrast between your and other people's view of the world will help you get along better with others, making room for who they are and directing them to positions in which they will work best.

Playful
How the Playful can create conflict with others

The Playful can get into trouble with others when they end up doing some tasks by the seat of their pants after not adequately preparing. They thus come across as unorganised. This is usually the result of leaving things until the last moment, and letting other things come in the way of what really needs to be done. Once something unexpected arises, Playfuls let other things build up to explosion point, then when there's too much pressure they abandon the cause entirely!

The Playful's habit of guessing rather than checking can also cause conflict with others. They tend to pull outlandish details from the sky, when a bit of research could give them some credibility. The Precise will have spent their precious time carefully mining for the right information, and labouring to get their presentation close to perfect. 'Why shouldn't the Playfuls try like I do?' the Precise would say. 'Near enough is not good enough!'

Frequently changing direction or going off on tangents without letting anyone know in advance is another way the Playful can cause conflict. This can come across as flippant and hugely frustrating, especially in meetings when others are trying to get something resolved. Acting impulsively can come across as impractical and not credible, especially to those task-driven types, the Precise and the Powerful, so Playfuls, sometimes you might have to ease up on your horsing around and light-hearted attitude.

Another major irritant is that Playfuls have so many stories, and want to do all the talking. Playfuls need to be aware of this habit, especially when they are at a meeting with a clear agenda. We don't have to hear them all! Defuse the conflict by making a conscious effort to listen.

How the Playful can frustrate others

For every personality, when we view things from only our perspective we can often frustrate others without realising it — and, for that matter, be frustrated by them. The Playful can drive other personalities senseless, especially the Precise and the Powerful. (They don't bother the Peaceful so much, as those types just ride out the bumps in life and are very accepting of others.)

Playfuls can frustrate others by being messy, noisy and always talking — and, from the Powerful/Precise perspective, making no sense at all. They seem to drift in and out of conversations, which for the Powerful and Precise is interpreted as disengagement, which is very disturbing to them. Powerful and Precise personalities are task-oriented and the Playful are people-oriented, so there lies an immediate source of great frustration.

The Playful's need for attention causes them to do things that really bother the Powerful and Precise. Their lack of attention to detail is also a bone of contention.

One of the biggest frustrations for others around the Playful is their lack of follow through. They volunteer for all sorts of things, but they can find execution and delivery hard to do. I'm not saying every Playful is like this, but they have to work hard in this area. The Playful's attitude to detail can cause others on their team to feel frustrated if they feel it's imperative that everyone understands what needs to be done.

Another Playful trait that can frustrate others is that they tend to talk in shorthand, not quite finishing their sentences. The Precise just shake their heads in exasperation and confusion — they need the full picture, which rarely gets expressed by the Playful.

Playfuls are often seen as shallow, but they would put up a strong argument against this. It's just that they are so into the 'fun' of life that they don't like being serious and held down.

How the Playful can feel frustrated by others
The Playful loves to play and have fun; to the Precise and Powerful, this is wasting time. If the Playful can't have play in their world they can lose motivation, and get frustrated by the person who is being the handbrake.

Powerful
How the Powerful can create conflict with others
Powerfuls can cause conflict when they shut down the conversation

at hand, either because it doesn't hold their interest, or the speaker is taking too long delivering the information. Powerfuls have a very good way of acting as if they are listening and attentive while their thoughts are elsewhere. That glazed look doesn't fool everyone, however, and some people can see right through it.

Powerfuls can also cause conflict by taking the floor all the time, and not letting others have their say. Often times the quieter types get fed up and shut down in passive resistance to the demands being made. Having strong, forceful types running everything can alienate other people and fragment a team.

Powerfuls, remember the small things, such as the 'please' and 'thank you' that you think you have said, but are forgotten because your mind is racing ahead at a hundred miles an hour. Also, think about your body language and how this might impact on others. Your commanding presence can intimidate.

No one else gets things done at the pace the Powerful goes at, so they shouldn't expect this of others. They need to ease up on being too demanding: the work will still get done. Powerfuls need to remember that when we are driven all the time, we get stressed, which causes burnout, blowout, and then walk out!

How the Powerful can frustrate others

The Powerful's formidable presence and questioning of the troops can force others — usually Peacefuls — to freeze on the spot when challenged. The Peacefuls then feel misunderstood, as they are much more capable than they may appear to the Powerful.

Powerfuls are circumstantial: they make their decisions on what is happening in the present. Precise types have this inclination as well, although they do consider the past strongly too. Playfuls also make decisions based on what's happening now, but are more focused on relationships, however, the Peaceful is not wired that way, and this can cause them to feel frustrated by the demanding Powerful.

How the Powerful can feel frustrated by others

Powerfuls, because of their ability to achieve, can quickly look at a situation and know how to best work around it. They can be highly frustrated by the other personalities, who don't see it quite like them. They are strongly results-driven, which is not a primary motivation for the other types.

Often a Powerful can be way out front, leading, then turn around and find no one is following. This results in them getting churned up, agitated, restless, impatient and bossy towards those who are in their way or dragging the chain.

They make quick decisions, and the tendency of others who have to think things over can also frustrate the Powerful.

Precise
How the Precise can create conflict with others

Precise personalities have a constant need to correct others, driven by their need to have things done 'right'. Unfortunately, because not everything can be done in the fashion the Precise requires, it's easy for them to withhold encouragement and praise, resulting in a despondent and discouraged team.

The Precise's deep need to provide data and information means they can come across as intense. This can frustrate those who aren't that way inclined. I know letting things go is difficult for the Precise, but they need to learn that they don't have to justify and explain why they did every little thing. Being so black and white can create conflict with others, especially when trying to work towards a group solution.

Because of their reluctance to divulge who they are on a personal level, Precise types can come across as remote, very private and self-contained. This can sometimes be interpreted as cool, distant and non-accepting of others, which can cause huge chasms between them and the other personality types.

Because Precises are so objective and task-oriented, this sometimes leaves no room for building any sort of personal relationship. So how can a Precise build a team when they give only the bare minimum of attention to this area? By easing up on being too particular, and being a little more open. Highly effective teams have a strong sense of openness and rapport.

How the Precise can frustrate others

The Precise can demotivate and frustrate the life out of others through their incredible insistence that things be correct, in order and sound. They think in objective terms, and won't let up if they believe they are right. It can feel like a terrier biting your ankle. And it's a double-edged sword; they get frustrated as well when others don't adhere to their high standards.

Their formal approach to everything makes them 'no-nonsense' types. The affable Playful can interpret this as the Precise not tolerating their hijinks, which can send them scurrying off in the opposite direction. The Precise's determination to present a library of data can turn off the Powerful, when all they want to do is get something done, not wait until its done perfectly. The Peaceful's strong attributes of perseverance and patience mean they just keep plodding on until the job's finished, unaffected by any of the external responses of a Precise.

How the Precise can feel frustrated by others

Because of their need to describe things fully, they feel immense frustration when they aren't given the opportunity to do this. They can also be frustrated when others don't see the need to try to fix things, and get them right. They love order, and don't tolerate those who don't.

Peaceful
How the Peaceful can create conflict with others

Despite their hatred of conflict, the Peaceful can actually cause it by not speaking up when they should. I know this often goes against who they are, and I know they'd rather just listen, but Peacefuls need to realise that not everyone else understands the way they make decisions. Taking their time can be interpreted as being uninvolved and indecisive.

Other personalities can react by pushing the Peaceful, which just causes them to dig in further, refusing to engage. Of course, they're often not aware that the Peaceful is doing this for some period of time, as Peacefuls can conceal this well. They are the 'nice' people on the block, so others can't imagine them consciously doing such a thing. If they only knew how strong Peacefuls really are (other terms could be stubborn, or a hidden will of steel). Peacefuls might not seek confrontations, but they can quietly resist when pushed.

How the Peaceful can frustrate others

The apparent low energy and lack of enthusiasm of a Peaceful can be a wet blanket for others. I often get told by those who work with these types, 'They're so hard to read.' There's not a lot of facial gestures, body language or outward enthusiasm.

Everyone agrees we need these calming types around us, but they can frustrate others with their low key, unenthusiastic, minimal-energy approach to most things.

In a conflict situation, its easy for Peacefuls to abandon the ship, pull away or stay under the radar. Alternatively, they might outwardly acquiesce but inside strongly resist. That is enormously frustrating to others.

The Peaceful's lack of fervour can really get a Powerful tetchy. Peacefuls would rather create a pleasant environment than move through life at a rapid pace. Powerfuls don't rate this high on their priority list. They are more concerned about results. So this pairing in the workplace is an accident waiting to happen if neither side knows how to relate to the other from their perspective and value their capabilities.

The Peaceful's favourite word is 'whatever'. They are tremendously obliging, and if you are not one of these types I'm sure you can see how this can make other personalities' blood boil. If you were to ask the other types what could make the relationship more collaborative, they would say, 'Peacefuls need to step up and be more decisive, more assertive.' Of course, it is not in their nature to be that way.

How the Peaceful can feel frustrated by others

Peacefuls can become frustrated by others when they don't feel valued or have respect shown to them. For a long time they are happy to have said nothing, done things in a low key way and finished all their tasks, but at the end of the day, they wonder if anyone cares.

This can be mildly frustrating for them, but they seldom wallow in frustration, as they are always subconsciously looking for ways to defuse stress and conflict. They pretty much nip it in the bud; it might be a fleeting thought, then they lay it down as quickly as they thought of it.

We can see how easy it is for an environment of frustration to be created when we don't understand the different personalities. A little insight into each of them can help to de-fuse the most frustrated person, as we begin to identify the triggers which set them off.

I am a great believer in focusing on people's strengths, and talents, but it is important to be aware of our frustrations and the way personalities react and respond to conflicts and stress.

12 The personalities in action

Once we know who we are, and are able to understand how other people are different, we can start to get our act together and work on creating a pathway through the work environment that is less stressful for ourselves and others. Let's look at some examples of how personalities can cause us to struggle in the workplace — and how to manage these situations.

In my work I meet lots of people and get many letters and emails from people asking for insight into dealing with those who are clearly different from them or, for that matter, those who are the same! You might identify with some of the following situations. You may have lived out some of them yourself. We face these kinds of scenarios in all of our work environments.

Remaining alert to the needs of others and creating an environment in which everyone can prosper doesn't have to be all that difficult. Organisations that learn about and use the personalities as part of their culture seem to forge ahead with fewer sick days (usually resulting from the stresses of working with people) and an atmosphere of collaboration and teamwork.

A Peaceful relating to a Powerful

A Peaceful wrote to me, anxious about handling a Powerful colleague at her team meetings. She continually felt invisible and under-valued, as her colleague tended to take over and undermine her.

This can be a big issue in the workplace, and I hear examples of it all too often. It's not that the Powerful want to cause tension; they are just operating out of the way they view their world, always ready to move in the moment, focusing on the task until completion. That's why they want everything done yesterday or, if that's not possible, immediately. Conversely Peacefuls have a tendency to sleep on things before acting, avoiding at all cost the tensions that may occur if they have to discuss an issue on the spot.

My response would be that this situation is very normal for Peacefuls — it's one of their major struggles in life. Keep in mind that from where the Powerful sits, the Peaceful can be as equally exasperating.

It's natural for Peacefuls to quietly resist in a passive way when goaded and pushed by demonstratively strong personalities. Peacefuls won't move if they don't want to, especially when hard-pressed. They smile and are gracious, but are surprisingly strong. The difference is that one type is internally strong (the Peaceful) and the other is externally strong, expressing and demonstrating their resistance (the Powerful).

We know that all too often, if a Powerful is operating out of their weaknesses (pushing their strengths to extreme), they become dictatorial and forget to appreciate others. They can make a Peaceful feel incompetent if they aren't following orders to 'Stand to attention and salute when I say'. Putting the Peaceful on the spot like this can make them freeze, go blank, and forget the question or subject they should be talking about. It can be very stressful for them.

The Powerful deduces from this that the Peaceful is indecisive, withholding information and is not a clear or sharp thinker. Generally that's enough for the Powerful to lose respect for them.

This is a shame, because if the Powerful used their brain they would see that by giving the Peaceful time to process with their brilliant listening skills (they can often pick up on stuff that the Powerfuls skip over), they would have on their team a very loyal, dedicated contributor who could add so much value to the outcomes. However, in meetings, Powerfuls have a natural penchant to get things going, and therefore step up to take control. They would rather speak than listen.

To overcome the frustration caused by these 'storm troopers' or 'generals' who want to take on the world every day, my suggestion is to table a clear agenda and set boundaries at the beginning. Each member is given a slot to speak with no interruptions — yes, that's right you Powerfuls, no interruptions — and then, once everyone has had their time slot, open discussion. Of course, part of the Peaceful's role is to come prepared to contribute so that time is not wasted.

Remember, Powerfuls want Peacefuls to speak in a more direct way. This is foreign to the Peaceful, as they avoid any type of communication that might provoke challenge or tension, and have a tendency to stretch things out, and pause more than the Powerful can stand. When communication doesn't move at the pace the Powerfuls want, their body language tells the Peaceful that they are bored, disinterested and restless, which causes the Peaceful to shut down. The difference between these two is that Peacefuls would prefer a still lake and the Powerful a rapid river. Make an effort to try to meet them at the end of the rapids at the beginning of the lake. Both scenes are breathtaking if we care to stop and look.

Peacefuls, remember when relating to a Powerful to be more hardy. Get right to business. Stick to the main points. Assert yourself more, and put more vigour and energy into what you say and do.

Pick up the pace, when walking and talking. Pause less, say what you think rather than what you feel, and address problems quickly.

When meeting with a Powerful, don't go over the allotted timeframe. They respect on-time completion. Don't relax until the job is completed.

Use time efficiently. Put decisions into operation as quickly as possible, and respond to emails immediately.

A Precise working with a Playful

It's not that I don't enjoy a joke or two — of course, everyone does — but honestly, I am at my wits' end having to work with a Playful on another project. They just keep horsing around. What I have noticed is their eagerness and willingness to volunteer themselves to work on different projects, but this fades quickly when they have to deliver the goods. Pinning them down for content, they have an uncanny way of quickly becoming elusive. When asked just how they are going to do something, they would rather tell me than give written data, which as far as I am concerned doesn't cut it, because we need written records to refer back to to monitor the process.

I am continually frustrated by their lack of respect for others. When we all make such an effort to be at various meetings on time, they come either unprepared or late.

It's not difficult to see how testing this situation could be for both parties. Playfuls want to have fun as they move through their tasks and projects. By fun, I mean developing relationships with those they are working with. Their idea of fun is creating memories of the event as they work through those tedious issues like research, planning and organising. This letter clearly showed me that this Playful hasn't given thought to who they are working with. So what would it take for everyone to be happy in this situation?

Firstly, Playfuls act and speak first, then think about it after, whereas Precises think things through before acting. That alone shows they are poles apart.

For the Precise, it's all in the packing a suitcase when going to some wonderful holiday destination. They put a lot of thought and effort into it and take it seriously. Ask a Playful how many times they go away and forget half the essentials!

Planning is life itself to these Precise ones. Groundwork is everything if they are going to face the obstacles up ahead. By being prepared, they can overcome most barriers and challenges. They strategically find ways to deal with all the pros and cons as they move forward and put in place resources to aid their success.

The Precise's idea of fun is a task completed with excellence, with minimal mistakes (preferably none). *Then* they will 'play'.

Do you see the difference? One plays as they go along, the other plays when the task is completed.

A smart collaborator will work within the two frameworks, for the good of everyone. We just need to take a moment to identify and acknowledge who is on the team and make room for their skills and strengths.

Playfuls don't mean to come unprepared, but the discipline of focusing on details or on one task at a time is not easy for them. However, they are great at networking with other support groups to serve the project. Their creativity and ability to come up with original concepts can really add value. The Precise's love of analysis and organisation can put these skills into action, by giving guidelines and putting processes in place for better outcomes.

The Precise need to accept that Playfuls want them to show personal interest in them. It is very important for Playfuls to engage with colleagues before they can work with them. From where the Playful sits, they see Precise types to be distant and somewhat cool and aloof, so they find it difficult to connect and build a rapport. Sharing a bit about who you are, or discussing something about others, will help break down the walls.

Because Playfuls love to talk quickly, are high-energy types, don't need a lot of detail and run with how they feel, these four aspects alone are totally alien to how a Precise would operate. Think about these facets and how you could apply them when next meeting with a Playful. The least you could do is talk about your different approaches to work, and how you can achieve the desired outcome together.

A Precise/Peaceful with a Playful/ Powerful boss

I am in middle management with a supervisor over me and approximately 30 people, including other department heads, under my supervision. My supervisor and I have worked together for 18 years, starting when the company was small and he was the only supervisor. I was promoted eight years ago to a job created to fill a need as the company grew.

Having grown with the company and been in the same field for 23 years, I feel I am very knowledgeable about my area and the outside factors that influence it. I also feel that I am very good at customer service and have the respect of the people we serve.

During the last few years my relationship with my boss has deteriorated. After learning about the personalities, I now have some insight as to why. My boss, a Playful/Powerful who likes to have his hand in everything that goes on, has had to pass on some responsibility to the department heads under him, due to company growth. Knowing that this makes him nervous, I am all too happy, with my Precise/Peaceful personality, to give him all the information so that he can make informed decisions. I give him lots of details, both pros and cons, but his Powerful side just wants the bottom line. Unfortunately, my critical skills, expressed through my reports over the years, have been viewed as me not being a team player. It just seemed like good business sense to me.

An example of this happened recently in a meeting with the boss and the other middle managers. He wanted the staff in my department to all stay past their contracted times to help our clientele. He wanted them to do it without pay, because if they believe in the company's vision, they should do this as part of the culture that has been established. I mentioned that the extra hours were not in their contracts. He didn't like that. I also asked what we should do about the extra money the staff would need for child care — shouldn't we at least cover that for them if we expect them to work overtime without pay? He said no. I repeated the scenario back to him, as one of the staff would view it. Of course it seemed ridiculous, but no one else at the table said a word. So he got mad at me.

I also never know if I am doing a good job or not. He will occasionally comment that I handled a situation well, and my yearly reviews are always good, but he never gives his middle managers the personal touch and kudos that he gives the rest of the staff.

I have been recently diagnosed with a health problem and have been depleted physically and not on top of my game for the last several months. I made the grave error of talking to my boss about it so that I could ask for some time off to recuperate.

Because of all of this, my boss views me as 'broken' and feels the need to 'fix' me. But he wants it done quickly, and done his way. So he has given me three weeks off, with several conditions, such as get your problem fixed, lose weight, see a counsellor etc. Some of these stipulations could be considered illegal if I wanted to go down that route, which I don't.

Unfortunately, after all these years, I am now seriously considering looking for another job. I am withering on the vine in my current position. I also feel ostracised by the other middle managers who don't want to make waves.

Here is someone who is not feeling valued and who, after giving more than 20 years to a company, feels ready to walk away, when understanding and working through these people issues could clear them up.

If only the Powerful could step back and view the world of the Peaceful/Precise, there could be some resolution here. The Peaceful/Precise wouldn't be so hurt by the Powerful's insensitivity to how loyal they have been. The Peaceful/Precise felt the need to objectively lay a situation out, and it was interpreted by the Powerful as a challenge. To add to the frustration, the silence from the Peaceful/Precise's colleagues made her feel isolated and a lone voice. Communication is not easy when you have a bunch of non-assertives and a strong Powerful on the team. It is a breeding ground for autocratic leadership, and that's where this situation is heading.

It would be interesting to hear an account of this same situation from the perspective of the Powerful. I'm sure they wouldn't have got into all that detail, and the hurt would not have been expressed. They don't tolerate sickness very well (Why? Because you can't produce when you're sick!). They would possibly justify the situation by saying that there are outcomes to achieve and the team needs to move forward quickly. Sometimes there are casualties, but that's business! They can steel themselves against the emotional side of issues. They also don't care too much if you don't like them. That is not an excuse, but sadly comes across as poor leadership.

It's a challenge when one person has begun to understand the different personalities and would like very much for the other person to see and understand their view of the world. Sadly, when this doesn't happen disappointment and discouragement seep in. It's obvious that this is the case here.

You can't just walk up to someone who doesn't know about the personalities and explain it to them, but there are some things you can do to create an environment in which to begin to work through some of these issues.

In this case, the Peaceful/Precise may have to step out of their comfort zone for a time, and try to communicate in a way that the Playful/Powerful will listen to. Yes, I know the two are poles apart, but to get some resolution it would be wise for the Peaceful/Precise to try to put themselves in the other position.

Sometimes Playful/Powerfuls are just so preoccupied with themselves and what they are doing, they can overlook the needs of their team. Their *tasks* are foremost in their minds. They can be building up their own bank balance of affirmation and recognition, and forgetting to bolster the troops'. Naturally the Peaceful/Precise would feel undervalued if that was the case. They are deliberate, courteous and self-deprecating, so they probably wouldn't put themselves 'out there', and consequently feel disappointed in the lack of acknowledgment towards them.

It's very hard for a Peaceful to address such up-front issues and it could backfire, especially when confronting someone as verbal as a Playful/Powerful. Their communication skills can really floor those who are more thinkers and prefer the written word. If you feel that you can't face this head on, perhaps resort to the written word — but still nothing long and drawn out; keep it short and to the point.

Although you are naturally a peacemaker, and it is awkward to address such issues, the Playful/Powerful will respect you more if you do. Initiate the contact. And remember, you don't have to stay in this place of assertiveness, just step into it to bring about a resolution.

A Precise with a Playful travelling companion

This was a simple task, but the outcome still makes me cringe when thinking about it. How can booking two train tickets to attend an out-of-town conference become such a fraught and stressful exercise? Apparently it's all in the different personality types, and now that I know I'm a Precise I understand why.

For me, booking train tickets should be a straightforward exercise made up of three logical, simple steps.

1. *Work out when we need to arrive.*
2. *Ascertain which train will get us there on time.*
3. *Make the reservation(s).*

My Precise nature wanted to focus on the facts, gain agreement and move on to the next task in a time and cost-effective way. Needless to say, it didn't work out that way.

Precise (me): The 7.20 train will get us there in good time to get across town and register without hitting rush-hour traffic. Shall I book the tickets?

Playful: I'd love to see *Les Misèrables* while we're in London. I wonder which theatre it's playing at?

Precise: [What? A show? You're thinking about down-time already?] Really? So I'll book three tickets for the 7.20 train then?

Powerful: No — Elaine will book my ticket. I'll be going straight from Oxford.

Precise: OK. So two tickets then? Do you want me to book a ticket for you [Miss Playful] on the same train?

Playful: A group of us went to see *Cats* in '98 and it was great. There was this awesome little Italian restaurant just round the corner from the theatre . . .

Precise: [Hello! Could you focus on the task in hand for a second? Trains? Tickets? Bookings?] OK. So are you going to be travelling with me?

Playful: Yes, of course! It'll be good to have some quality time to chat and really catch up, eh?

Precise: [I don't think so! Two hours on a train is a perfect opportunity to catch up on some reading. Haven't you seen my in-tray? And anyway, I've no doubt you'll be doing all the talking . . .] Actually, I'm planning on reading Dave's report and some other bits and pieces to make good use of the time.

Playful: Dave's report? Oh yeah . . . Well, if you read it and fill me in on the essential bits I'll focus on how we can have some fun in the capital! You know what they say, all work and no play . . .

Precise: [You want me to do the hard work then brief you? Are you serious? Do I really have to travel with you?] So the 7.20 train works for you?

Playful: The last time I was at Paddington Station I remember there was this really great busker playing the mouth-organ and juggling plates. He drew quite a crowd. A young guy, but really talented. I wonder what he's doing now?

Precise: [Puh-leeez! What part of 'Does this work for you' don't you understand? I'll give you a clue — the answer is either 'Yes' or 'No'] 7.20. Train. You want me to book?

Playful: I've often wondered why people don't talk to each other on trains. It's the perfect opportunity to meet new and interesting people, don't you think?

Precise: [Hand to forehead. Why did I say yes to this trip? It's already a nightmare! All I wanted to know was 'Shall I book two tickets?'] Hey, you know what? I've got to run. How about I give your PA a call and she can book the ticket for you?

Playful: That would be great, thank you! She's so organised. Just like you! I don't know what I'd do without her.

Precise: [shakes head and mutters under breath]

If only I'd understood then how different personality types act and respond, I'd have handled things quite differently and had a much less frustrating experience. A little understanding goes a long way and enables us to modify our behaviour and responses so that we enjoy, rather than endure, the experience.

Now when I interact with someone who demonstrates a Playful, Peaceful or Powerful personality type, I make a conscious effort to understand their needs while meeting mine in the process. Precise!

I smiled when I received this, as it clearly illustrated an 'a-ha' moment for the Precise! Admitting they might have handled things differently shows that sometimes we can't go full steam ahead but need to consider the person we are relating too, otherwise we just won't get buy-in from others. Modifying our personalities so that we move closer to those opposites in our lives can help.

The Precise definitely wanted to maximise their time spent

travelling — they value and respect time — whereas the Playful was just enjoying the journey and definitely wanting some fun in the process.

So remember Playfuls, instead of sharing all your stories, perhaps listen more to the Precise. Consider them. Be polite instead of being so impulsive — and quieten down. Think about how you are going to do something rather than just going in like a bull in a china shop. I know directions and describing things is not your strength, but try your best. I am sure the Precise will respect you more if you do.

Precise, because you think more than you speak, you can often make Playfuls uncomfortable as they don't know what you think or feel about them. It's important that they feel accepted and approved of. Sometimes by your remoteness you make them feel less intelligent and capable. You take power from them when you do.

Peaceful leader with a Powerful team member

This is a long one, but it is important that I leave it as is, as it is such a clear example of conflicting personalities in action. Stay with it!

I work as an activities officer at a respite centre, caring for aged people who are at risk of social isolation in the community. My job is to provide meaningful activities as well as social interaction in the respite centre environment.

As the activities officer, I have a number of volunteers to help put the plans into action. Many of the volunteers have been with the organisation for over 20 years, and many have been there since the inception of the group.

I came into this organisation as the first activities officer employed by the government agency. The new management felt that the programmes, previously run by volunteers, had no direction, that they were boring and that the clients needed to be provided with programmes that were interesting, stimulating and a lot of fun.

On my first day I walked into a minefield. A meeting was planned half an hour before the programme was to commence, so that I could introduce myself to the volunteers and give them some ideas of what the day was

126

going to hold and get some feedback and ideas from them. The first thing I was greeted with was, 'Well, what are you going to do that we weren't already doing?' I told them that I had extensive experience working as a diversional therapist and that I was looking forward to building on what they had already established. I explained that I had run a lot of programmes by myself in my previous employment as I had never had a large volunteer base to work with. Ann [not real name] burst in immediately with the response, 'Well, you can do it yourself then.' I told her, 'Yes, I could do it myself, but that is not what I am here for. I am here to coordinate all our ideas and to have you all having input into the programme.'

When I started to outline the day's programme, Ann (a Powerful) talked over the top of me and asked if I was the coordinator. I understood that the coordinator title belonged to my boss, so I said, 'No, I am not the coordinator, I am the activities officer.' Ann then asked me, 'Do you have authority to make decisions?' I replied, 'I can make most decisions regarding running the programme for this group, but there are things I would have to run past the manager, as a courtesy.'

This was not good enough for Ann. Every meeting thereafter, Ann would come up with a curly scenario to see if I had the authority to deal with it. When I would reply, 'Well, I'd have to speak to the manager about that', she would just roll her eyes and say, 'Aren't you the coordinator around here?' I always felt as though I had been dragged through the mill after those morning meetings — before the programme even began!

At one meeting we decided to have a fashion parade for the clients' entertainment. We decided that the volunteers and I would get dressed up in clothes from the op shop that operated at the centre. We decided that we would model day wear, evening wear, and anything else that would raise a laugh. Ann said she wasn't going to model anything, but she would be the compère. Well, that sounded fair enough, so she was given that job.

On the day of the fashion parade, all the models got together and placed their clothes in the order of the programme and waited behind the scenes for the compère to call them out. We all came out one at a time and walked around the clients and 'strutted our stuff'.

When I came out, Ann described my outfit and then rushed up to me and lifted the back of my dress up so everyone could see my underwear. I was stunned initially, but I knew that the clients loved me and they knew *that Ann was behaving badly, so I made a joke of it and said, 'Yes, even my pants are colour-coordinated!'*

I was back in the changing room putting on my next set of clothes when some of the volunteers told me that Ann had changed the whole format of the fashion parade. She had decided that the clients didn't want to watch us, but that they wanted to be in the fashion parade themselves. So she was calling people up to her podium, at random, and telling them, 'You're looking beautiful today, tell us about what you are wearing.' She then completely sabotaged the fashion parade by getting the clients to walk around the room and show off their clothes while I watched in horror and tried to absorb what was happening. I thought, we are meant to be client-focused so I'll let this go on for a few minutes and then I'll need to tell her that we have models dressed ready to go out. Ann just kept on going, even though I was trying to make eye contact with her to wind it up. I didn't really want to go out all dressed up in my next outfit and tell her to close that segment, but eventually I had to do it, otherwise time would run out and the fashion parade wouldn't be finished. Ann ignored me for quite some time and kept on calling up clients to model their ordinary clothes. I was quite exasperated with her. Eventually Ann got back to the programme, but time had almost run out. The models only had the barest amount of time to scoot around the room and show off their clothes before the programme time had ended and the bus driver was ready to take the clients home.

After the programme I spoke to Ann and told her that she should have run that segment past me, if that was what she had planned to do. She retorted, 'The programme is for the clients, so I gave them an opportunity to be centre stage.' I told her that this was for their entertainment, and that we could have run a client fashion parade at another time for them. It was like water off a duck's back, and she showed no regret for her actions.

I felt I didn't know what to do with her. She was a law unto herself. She was very vocal in the group and the other volunteers would not stand up to her, even though she had inconvenienced them too. She was very powerful in the group and always followed her own agenda.

I love my job but I hate this Powerful who has never considered anyone but herself!

Can you see how this Peaceful wanted collaboration from the group? She wanted to have everyone's buy-in and was willing to spend a lot of her time (even outside her working hours) building a strong team. She explained her position and what she wanted to achieve, making sure everyone understood, but that wasn't enough for the Powerful.

The Powerful wanted to be in the control seat, and worked to that end. Fighting the battle, but not winning the war!

Peacefuls are very good at one liners, and she came back to win the heart of the audience.

Because the Peaceful would rather not start a conflict, they quietly pull back but passively resent the situation. The Peaceful was the casualty here because the Powerful had no insight into people skills.

Interestingly, I gave this letter to another Powerful to read, and she lost interest before she had finished the first page! Her reaction? 'Too long-winded. S*** happens. Get over it!'

A Peaceful/Precise bringing balance to a team

It was at the NZMBA [New Zealand Mortgage Brokers Association] conference in Christchurch that I first got to enjoy your session on fostering relationships. I'd been to similar sessions putting people into quadrants but I often found that I'd misread someone's personality. Your simple tool on the quadrant has been invaluable.

Shortly after the conference we needed to employ a PA, and as part of the employment process we got the final applicants to fill in your chart and circle how they saw/rated themselves. We narrowed it down to three applicants from our initial meetings; all were very qualified, charming, just what we were looking for. It turned out that we had misread two applicants, however. Their personalities were Powerful, which wouldn't have worked in our office environment, looking at the make up of who was already there. We needed a balance of all types, and we already had too many Powerfuls.

Needless to say, we employed the applicant who was mainly Peaceful/Precise, who is still with us today. We continue to use this simple form when employing and haven't missed yet. Thank you.

There is some debate about using personality tools to hire people. Even if you carefully choose a balanced team, you can have opposites really frustrated by each other. The secret is in knowing how the personalities work and appreciating everyone's capabilities.

A well-balanced team certainly can lift performance and productivity, if everyone knows and appreciates each other's strengths. Putting them in positions where they thrive would help enormously.

If I were interviewing, I probably would rather look for clues from the behaviour the applicant was displaying, and work from there.

- Are they loud, or do they have a softly spoken way about them?
- Are they direct, or do they talk around issues?
- Are they demonstrative, or are they more deliberate in what they do?

The different personalities bring the following strengths to a team.

- Playful — creativity, ideas and innovation
- Powerful — assertion and keeping on track
- Precise — organisation and process
- Peaceful — diplomacy and clarity.

It is good that this organisation understood they needed to bring a Peaceful/Precise on board to bring balance to an already top-heavy Powerful team.

Here is a further example of how understanding the strengths of different personalities has fostered a positive business environment.

A Powerful/Playful and a Peaceful/Precise

This is exemplified by the working relationship I have with my office administrator, which has been in place now for ten years. I am a Powerful/ Playful and my administrator is a Peaceful/Precise (generally not attention-seeking types — she consequently wouldn't let me use her name for this example). She has great attention to detail and very good organisational skills. This can not be better highlighted than with the simple workings of the office computer.

On numerous occasions I have asked her to help me with some technical aspect of the computer. The usual response is, 'James, have you bothered to read the instructions?' To this I reply, 'Look, don't give me that detail rubbish, I just want to do X, Y, Z.' Basically, I just want it to happen and happen now, not worrying about all the finer 'rubbish' which seems to me to be insignificant, mundane details. This is a classic example of myself in the Powerful/Playful role wanting to get to the crux of the matter and not having the time, patience or inclination to actually work through the procedures which are required for computer operations. This is as opposed to a Powerful/Precise, who would have no issues at all with this as they find the details and workings behind things quite interesting and have no problem dealing with regimented and technical systems.

This aspect is also very important when organising functions. A simple example is when I took a group of employees to an off-site workshop at a health spa. I presented a two-day forum but all the organising and detail behind the scenes was achieved by my office administrator. She was quite happy to have a lower profile and get all the details in place for the smooth running of the operation, as opposed to myself who really just wanted to get there and get started.

Often in these cases I tend to wing it, because I don't have too much interest in fluffing around with a lot of preparatory information. However, this is one trait that I have had to unlearn. Things go better if they are well researched and presented with a certain amount of organisation. This goes against the grain of a Powerful/Playful but this is a necessary evil.

This endorsement came from an up-and-coming personality convert. James has taken these concepts on board, and I love listening to him and the stories he tells.

His PA is brilliant at finishing off tasks. In all the time that I have done training in this organisation, I have never known her to forget anything that I needed. I can be confident that everything is ready and waiting, every time. She is very reliable.

She doesn't seek the limelight, is a delight to be around, and is a valuable member of James' team. James is such a big-picture person, he relies heavily on the details being completed by his PA. This is a great workable team as he knows what he is better at doing, and if he gives his PA the praise and appreciation she deserves, this could go from strength to strength.

Of course, it doesn't hurt us to work on improving our weaknesses. But there is an art in gathering a team with different capabilities and strengths to you.

A team of Powerful/Precise executive managers with a Peaceful/Precise CEO

This mix was a disaster waiting to happen. Yes, they achieved a lot, but to go the distance this top-heavy team of six Powerful/Precise personalities in management positions felt the frustration of having to deal with their CEO, a Peaceful/ Precise.

While they all had commonality with their Precise sides, focusing on outcomes and goals, their Powerful and Peaceful sides were poles apart.

The diplomatic CEO kept everything on an even keel, but this drove the Powerful/Precises nuts, as they felt they were being held back on things they saw could be achieved 'now!'

'Let's just do it,' they'd say. He would reply, 'If it still sits well in a few days' time, then we will move on this.'

In their meetings you could cut the air with a knife, the tensions evident. The Powerfuls' body language expressed their impatience and restlessness. Typically, the Peaceful CEO was not impacted by these external signals that the Powerfuls gave off. He was always able to ride the storms that came his way. His diplomatic, mediative leadership style absorbed the bun fights that often occurred in meetings, settling down the action-packed 'do it now' types. He never seemed threatened by these fearless types who were constantly verbalising their dissatisfaction.

When I went back in six months' time, four of the six executive managers had left — probably to a position where they could assert their authority. It was interesting to observe that the Peaceful/Precise CEO did achieve the required outcomes, but in a timeframe that was more conducive to him than to the team of Powerfuls.

Of course, you can see how this would have frustrated them. Peacefuls are very good at dampening down tempers, and this CEO had the ability to quieten the storms that seemed to rage with the keen Powerfuls on his team. Perhaps if he had considered how he could have utilised the energy of the Powerful/Precises by giving them special projects to complete, he may well have kept them on the team.

We all are aware of the costs involved in training someone for a senior position, and it's a pity that so many of them left when all it would have taken to retain them was some insight into what made them fizz.

Powerful with another Powerful

The sales manager where I work is a very strong Powerful, who always needs to be right and in control. Well, a few years ago we hired a gentleman to work on our order desk. It turned out that Graham, the new order desk guy, was also a strong Powerful. He works so hard, is usually right and does do a really good job. He is trying his best to develop in his career, but because of the Powerful sales manager's desire to be in control, he is not allowing Graham to spread his wings and fly. He doesn't want anyone to be better than him and to lose control of people, so he is holding back a really great employee who could turn out to be a star.

I am guessing this scenario was being observed by a Peaceful or Precise — most likely a Precise who cares strongly for justice!

An important lesson for a Powerful

One expression of the Powerful personality trait is they can look too much at the big picture only and ignore smaller issues, even though they do not consciously downplay the significance of them. This is a lesson I learnt very early on, in my first job as a relieving manager at a hotel in Dunedin.

I was in my early 20s, extremely keen to get the task done to the best of my ability and create a good impression in my new chosen career. In my first role as a duty manager I worked extremely long hours, sometimes between 80 and 100 hours a week. This included various roles from helping to clean to locking up at night, which could be at 1 or 2 a.m., then be up again at 6.30 a.m. to help serve breakfast. I worked hard and played hard as people in the hospitality industry do. I thought I was polite to my staff and always believed I had thanked them for the tasks they undertook.

However, I had a rude awakening from one of the senior bar staff regarding this. This man, a long-standing employee and barman at the Law Courts, called me aside, saying, 'Lad [more as a term of endearment], there is something you need to be aware of.' He then proceeded to tell me that all the staff were right behind me with my enthusiastic approach and hard work, 'but a little word goes a long way.' My response was a rather bemused look, and I rather naively replied, 'What do you mean?'

'Well, a little word called thanks goes a long way.'

My initial response was defensive and somewhat astonished. I was certain that I always thanked the staff as a common courtesy and good manners. I explained this to him, saying that I thought I always did say thanks, and his reply was, 'Well, as I said, lad, we are right behind you but it is being noticed by most of the staff that you don't take the time to thank them for their efforts.'

I greatly appreciated that he had taken the time to tell me this in an appropriate manner, away from other staff, in an advisory role, rather than as a complaint. He was doing it to help develop my people management skills.

This is one lesson that I have never forgotten, and is an example of how Powerful personality types can be so engrossed in the big picture that they fail to see the little things, even though as I have stated before they do not place any less importance on them.

I frequently hear staff bemoaning the fact that their Powerful boss doesn't even acknowledge them. Powerfuls don't intentionally do this — they are just preoccupied with other, more pressing things. This doesn't apply to all Powerful bosses, but a lot can come across in a way that makes others on their team feel invisible when they are around.

The Powerful can be so engrossed in their task that they forget to acknowledge others. Saying 'Please' and 'Thank you' goes a long way to motivate people. Powerfuls can be astounded when someone suggests they might like to acknowledge a job well done — they probably think they have said it, but it's more a thought than expressed outwardly.

Powerfuls also feel that they would rather acknowledge tasks well done by people who have gone the extra mile. Just *doing* something isn't worthy of praise to these types.

A helpful reminder here, you Powerfuls. There is nothing more motivating than when your boss tells you how valuable you are. For the Powerful and Precise, that value would have to come from what they do. For the Peaceful and Playful, that value would have to come from who they are.

There is a difference. If you want to hit the target, start from here.

Personalities in the wrong roles

Our receptionist had quit and they hired a young girl to replace her but the only problem was she was a Precise! You do not put a quiet, reserved, drained-by-people type out there to be your front desk superstar. You are setting the poor thing up for failure before she has a chance.

When the customers came in she didn't talk to them, was not very friendly on the phone and had a hard time dealing with the whole idea of being 'up front'. Guess what . . . she quit as well. She was so reliable, so dependable and her paperwork was amazing. They lost a really great employee simply because they didn't understand the strengths and weaknesses of her personality type and didn't place her where she would have thrived.

In one of our departments at work, there are four people with a supervisor named Joel. Joel was pushed into this position and is not rising to the occasion very well. He is a very strong Peaceful and really doesn't care one way or the other about being a supervisor. He does not know how to call a meeting or talk to any of the other staff when a challenging situation arises, and is finding himself feeling a lot of stress these days. No wonder

— they need a leader, a dynamic leader who will show them the vision and inspire them, not someone who really doesn't care.

Joel told me that he just wants to come to work, do his job and go home. Spoken like a true Peaceful! If only they would allow him to work out of his strengths he would probably stay there forever. Peacefuls are very loyal employees but from where I sit, if they don't stop pushing him, they could lose him entirely.

This second example is a case of a Peaceful not wanting to be left carrying the can. He obviously prefers not to lead.

I have met Peacefuls who lead extremely well. They have picked up the gauntlet and are very good at building a team around them who have different capabilities from them. That's when it really works.

Perhaps in both these situations, higher-ups should have looked more closely at the employee's personality and chosen their role more carefully, as in the next couple of examples.

Staff selection through understanding personalities

Since attending Allison's Personality Plus courses a number of years ago, I keep the fundamentals of this programme in mind when selecting staff, either for promotion or for initial employment.

I believe the key attribute of any staff member, and my main criterion for employment, is attitude. The application of each person's individual attitude or their expression of it is easier to notice, define and understand when you take into account the guidelines offered by Allison's programme of the four various types of personalities.

A good example of this in practice is in my role of managing 90 predominantly female flight attendants, based in seven regions around New Zealand. I must have confidence in these staff when managing them from afar, and the attitudes and abilities of these people is key when selecting a supervisor to be in charge of each of the bases. I assess the staff in each base, look at their strengths and weaknesses, whether they are an outgoing group, unorganised or regimented, and this helps to determine the selection of the supervisor.

If a base appears to be lacking structure, discipline and organisation, I automatically tend to select somebody with a Powerful/Precise personality. People with these traits tend to have a good combination of leadership skills combined with the ability to organise, adding structure and stability to the base. This helps bond them together as a team.

Conversely, if I have a base full of predominantly Precise/Peaceful personality types I will always select a Powerful/Playful personality type as a manager. They add a bit of spark to the group and help to draw out the individual attributes of the other flight attendants, as well as organise social functions and again enhance the team dynamic.

The selection process is even more clear cut when I am selecting for the role of ground course instructor. These people conduct the initial training of our flight attendants. This role always involves a pair of instructors, and I ensure that they are a good mix of Playful and Precise personalities. This helps to provide a far more complete and rounded training programme for the trainee flight attendants. The Playful personality instructor tends to draw out the more outgoing personalities and expand on their customer service skills. However, to give this balance I also ensure that I have a Precise personality instructing because of the regimentation and strict adherence to procedures required for the flight attendant role. The Precise personality type in this training role focuses on the detail and always ensures that people are punctual, well-groomed and, most importantly, have an excellent knowledge of the safety and regulatory requirements of the programme. This helps balance the more flamboyant, 'out there' personality of the other instructor.

The end result of this is the ground course develops trainees with a good balance of people and organisational skills.

It really excites me when I hear of how someone from a strong customer-driven organisation has picked up the concepts of personalities, and found value in strategically hand-picking the right staff for certain positions. This person has seen the value in a well-balanced team, and where there is a strong emphasis on one type, he has purposefully looked at an opposite to complement the team. I am confident staff retention and sick days would be minimal, looking at the dynamics of this well thought-out and well-chosen team.

After hearing you talk about the personalities, when I was restructuring I took heed of your suggestion about finding all four types for the team.

I chose a Powerful/Playful to head the sales team because I knew I could depend on them to drive the team. Being both people- and task-driven helped them with customer relationships as well as keeping our sights on where we needed to go. I had them also working on the development side of the business.

I chose a Precise/Powerful combination as the financial controller. He was a definite benefit to us as an organisation. His love of analysis showed each time we had our monthly meeting, we could see what our expenditure was, supported it with graphs and charts, and could forecast what was required for the next cycle, as well as keeping costs down.

While he could frustrate those Playfuls in the sales team by insisting on having their sales reports in on time, we could be sure that at the hit of a computer key we could access the sales targets immediately. He went over every sales person's chits and receipts with a fine-tooth comb and therefore very rarely did I see him have to repeat or re-do things.

The best thing I did was giving him his own office. This was by default, but it worked. He loved the quiet, peaceful surroundings so he could get his head around the nuts and bolts of whether we would be making a profit or not. I appreciated his love of analysis and his ability to interpret what was foreign to me. He was never a threat but a complement to the business.

The Playful receptionist was an outstanding asset to the company, always cheerful and bright, and never complaining about the many phone calls and interruptions to her day. She treated the clients as good friends. Her ability to make everyone who walked through the door special made light our own work. She was the face of our company, and a huge advantage to it.

The Peaceful/Precise could be counted on to process all the administrative tasks, and have things finished on the due date. Their calming way had a de-stressing effect on the team. Their dry wit came through and broke the tensions that come with running a business.

Our team meetings showed the different strengths that each brought to the company. Understanding this has helped us to draw from each other's strengths, and no one feels threatened by the abilities of the others. We occasionally have a good laugh at ourselves when the irksome side of us shows. No-one gets heated, because we have learnt to appreciate the strengths we all have.

The comments from this organisation endorse the absolute importance of working with a diverse group of capabilities and personalities. The decision-makers have given a fair amount of thought as to which personality would suit which role.

Placing each of the personalities in a role that allows them to operate out of their strengths makes for workplace harmony. This is evident in this medium-sized business.

13 Pressing the right buttons at home

I believe being happy at work has a huge bearing on what is happening at home, and vice versa. So often we separate the two spheres, but I have discovered that each person's underlying personality traits and behaviours want to be expressed in both places. If they are held down or masked in either environment, over time it becomes uncomfortable in each place, resulting in stress.

Think of those you live with. Maybe you fell in love with a man who was deeply sensitive and had a wonderful knack for doing things properly. Several years into the relationship he's driving you crazy by insisting that the toilet roll be loaded onto the holder the right way — again!

While there's no doubt that opposites attract, isn't it amazing how the qualities that initially attracted us to a mate are the same ones that end up driving us to distraction?

But there's a simple key to understanding and resolving your frustration, and it's realising that often it's the differences between partners that make a relationship interesting, invigorating and ultimately long-lasting. What they are is what you need in your life, and what *you* are is what *they* need!

Essentially, the same insight into personalities that can help us at work can also be used to help us understand ourselves and our partners in the home environment. It's not about putting someone into a box or categorising them, it's simply a way that you can communicate with them more effectively and best relate to them. One of the pivotal things to learn in a relationship is how to relate to our partner according to their perspective, rather than ours. But more often than not we do the opposite: relate from how we see our world.

Everyone comes with different strengths, but each personality type also comes with accompanying weaknesses. In practical terms, that means a Playful's ability to effectively communicate turns into an annoying inclination to talk too much when out of balance. Powerfuls are born leaders, but when pushed to the extreme they default to becoming dictatorial and tyrannical. Those brilliant, organised Precise types can quickly become finicky and pedantic when out of balance. Peacefuls, who are excellent listeners with a fantastic dry sense of humour, simply don't say anything. You can imagine how frustrating that can be when their partner wants a response.

Just because those behaviours are driving you crazy, is that a reason to get out of the relationship? No way! Discovering the differences between personalities is not a licence to quit. It's about being aware and tolerant of where your spouse is coming from.

In relationships, we need to bring those differences to the table because that's what helps us push each other to new levels, grow together and have greater respect for each other's strengths.

It is so important to understand how each personality type views their world, then we can make adjustments to communicate with them. Otherwise:

- Powerfuls can be exasperated by the Peacefuls' indecisiveness
- Precises can drive Playfuls away with their intense need to get things right
- Peacefuls can become passive-aggressive as they get inwardly 'ticked off'
- Playfuls will start to do anything to get attention.

It is worth noting that falling in love with someone who is the same personality type as you doesn't necessarily mean a hassle-free path to a happily-ever-after future. If both of you are the same, in fact you have to work a little bit harder.

It might be nice at the beginning, but can you imagine two Playfuls in one house? They both want to be the star and the one in the limelight, so they look at the other person and say 'Don't steal my thunder! I want the applause!' Another trait is that they're not very detail-driven or orderly, so over time chaos builds in their home (and neither of them can ever find their keys!).

Two Powerfuls in the home are interesting because they both want to take control and be the boss. Again, nice at the beginning, because they can talk at ease about productivity and results . . . but over time they get into conflict as they both want their ideas administered and achieved.

Two Precise types living together would be constantly reviewing their checklists, making sure everything has been done before they relax for the evening. They love structure, detail and organisation, but their serious nature and no-nonsense behaviour could limit fun in the home, as they are focused on strategising and getting tasks accomplished, and would be correcting each other on a continual basis.

Meanwhile, two Peacefuls will look at each other and one will say, 'What do you want to do?' The other will say, 'I don't know — what do you want to do?' 'Whatever.' As you can see, nothing happens or gets accomplished.

That is not to say that two people of the same type can't make a relationship work, but remember that both of you may have to work harder at the things neither of you are motivated to do!

Understanding different personalities at home goes beyond getting on with our significant other. As I said earlier in the book, often our children are very different from us, too. Here are two excellent examples.

I first met Allie at a Women In Business evening where she was our guest speaker. This meeting was to completely change the way I interacted with people forever. Firstly, I could immediately understand why it was that my eldest son Kyle, a beautiful Peaceful, and my husband Graeme, a total Powerful, often struggled to understand each other, with conflict often the outcome . . .

For myself personally, Personality Plus has been a wonderful tool to have. I am able to more easily relate to my two sons, Kyle the Peaceful and Kim the Precise. I have to say the best is the fact that I now understand Graeme. After 30 years of marriage we now have a deeper love and understanding of each other.

It felt as though he was always trying to dominate me, push me to do what he thought I should be doing and should be asking him for permission to do it. I am a Peaceful/Precise; in other words, I spend most of my time in the Peaceful until I am really tired and then I revert to the Precise and get frustrated if things are not done just so. For Graeme I was at times annoying as I would be quietly doing my thing, at my pace, yet this would not be fast enough or outgoing enough for him.

I have now learnt to be myself and am able to be amongst people I do not know and talk with ease, knowing my strengths and knowing I am not wrong to be a Peaceful. I love it!

After I presented to a large audience in Whangarei, Northland, I asked if anyone had any questions or comments. A Powerful gentleman stood up and said the following.

Thank you. You have tonight put a language around something really important. I have known this in part, but tonight the language has never been more clear.

If you asked those people who know me, they would say I am very well respected in this town because of what I have accomplished. A captain of industry, you might say. I've always enjoyed working, and this has grown out of my drive to get things done. When I was growing up, I naturally grew into leadership roles: head prefect, in the First XV, team captain, just to name a few.

I would consider myself very successful in commerce, but I consider myself a failure at home. This failure is with my 17-year-old son. He has stopped really talking to me. In fact, I would say he's pulled down the blind on any nurturing relationship with me.

This has come about by my own doing. Over the years I have provoked him to get out there and join a sports team. I come home from work and find him lying on the couch, watching TV and eating. Just looking at him lying around, I get stirred up and angry. My first reaction is to say, 'What have you done today?'

Tonight you have painted a picture of him and I locking heads because of my preoccupation about making him like me. You suggested he might be a Peaceful, and I realised tonight that I haven't filled up his tank for years. It's so foreign to me. Giving respect and value — how can I do this when he doesn't do anything that would earn my respect? No wonder he doesn't try to make any conversation with me anymore. No wonder I have no relationship with him — he doesn't feel significant or valued.

As a Powerful, and with him a Peaceful, you have made me see that we look at the world differently. I want to be known for what I do, and it seems he wants to be known for who he is.

I might just go home and do it differently.

I was floored that this Powerful could admit this in a room full of people!

I had a phone call from him the next day and he described what he did when he got home that night (yes, that night. No Powerful wants to wait until the morning!).

I walked into my son's room. This was 10.30 p.m. and he was sleeping. I shook him awake, and while he was rubbing his eyes and trying to wake up, my son said, 'What's up, Dad, is there a fire or something? What's the urgency?' I proceeded to tell him what I had discovered that night.

'Son, tonight I have discovered a compelling tool that has got me thinking about our relationship. I can see I bother you by the way I do things and what I require from you. I make demands, and I can see you pulling away as you would prefer to be asked rather than told. I have never given thought to the way you see your world, or the fact that you create a harmonious environment — always obliging your mother, and not reacting to what is thrown at you, mostly by me.

Your steady, balanced way certainly helps in the family dynamic. Never

144

getting hassled, always reliable. I started thinking about how much you mean to me. The patience you have displayed by waiting for me to come home to hang out with you, when other pressing issues were addressing me at work . . . I wouldn't have waited around like you have . . . '

And guess what? Their conversation continued way into the night about some of the ways that he had missed the mark, and how they had missed hanging out together. Throughout this encounter his son looked him in the eye and showed acceptance. The cold wall that had been built between them was dissipated, just by that Powerful father filling the tank of his Peaceful teenager.

People pay huge amounts of money for therapy seeking this kind of communication and dialogue, when all it takes is understanding the different personalities.

Conclusion

No excuses!

As the first part of this book comes to a close, I hope you have a greater understanding of yourself and others. I have written each page from the heart, knowing the huge impact this subject matter has had on my life, with the desire that it will do the same for you.

No matter which personality type you are, there are probably some parts of it that you feel are not you, because of the way you have been raised, and the influence of others who have helped develop you. Remember that these are all generalisations, and take from them what you feel pertains to you. But be honest with yourself, and use this tool to further develop who you are. It is a powerful tool that has the ability to grow extraordinary people.

A word of caution, however: please don't close this book and start categorising people. When I first discovered this tool, I did this, and it put people off. I remember going home with this imaginary piece of four by two over my shoulder, excitedly telling my husband who he was. Can you imagine how a Peaceful embraced that? He was polite, but it took about six months before he picked up a book about it. How ignorant on my part!

Also, it would be easy to close this book and say, 'Well, that's just the way I am', then use that as an excuse not to work on minimising those traits of yours that can bother others. Let me encourage you to regularly take stock of how you might come across to others, and continue to work at how you can diminish those aspects of your personality and behaviour that can frustrate others.

The hot issues today in business are staff retention, skill shortages, disputes in the workplace, cultural issues. Can you see the value of considering personalities in these areas? It is a key component for business success.

If you are a boss, hopefully you now have clearer insights into your staff, and how to get the best out of them. Getting into their shoes and looking at the world from where they sit will help you to understand them, with the sole purpose of developing them according to their capabilities and strengths. If you do this, you'll be a boss who never will be forgotten.

For those on the shop floor dealing with customers, there is no doubt this tool will improve your company's bottom line. When you can relate and sell according to personality, you will find improved customer retention.

If you do not yet have a leadership role, hopefully you can now see how your personality has the ability to lead, so you can start taking incremental steps towards being all that you were designed to be.

Observe the behaviours of others so you can identify the different types on your team, and discuss ways of using their natural personality strengths for the common good. Meetings can be a frustrating experience if you don't know how to work with people and move towards agreement. This is the best tool I know to help you do that.

Remember the three hungers of humankind mentioned earlier in the book.

1. To connect with the creative energy that infuses all of life.
2. To know and express our talents.
3. To know that our lives matter, and that we will leave behind some kind of legacy.

I can't think of any other tool that will help you achieve this. I am confident that using the principles described in this book will result in happier, more fulfilled people working in teams that respect each other's differences, and use this framework to connect.

There is no doubt in my mind that your staff retention rate will soar as you begin to actually enjoy your colleagues and work with them according to their personalities, and I guarantee you will experience added benefits as it flows into your personal life as well.

'People are normal, until you get to know them', so the saying goes. I say, 'People are normal until you get to know them through their personalities, and when we start relating to them from how they view their world, they become extraordinary.'

So what is the best personality? The one that is operating out of its strengths! Remember, no one personality is right or wrong — they are all just different.

Start pressing the right buttons, and see where it takes you.

Quick reference guide

Here is a quick reference guide, based on Florence and Marita Littauer's work, on how each personality reacts to many of the issues we face each day in business. Sometimes we just don't have time to read a whole book, or we just need to look up the relevant information. When you want a quick answer to a challenging situation, this part of the book will help you find it easily.

As you flick through you will be able to address the issue at hand, with some immediate clues as to how to deal with whatever is pressing your button or that of a member of your team.

A–Z index

AFRAID OF . . .

PLAYFUL	POWERFUL
Not being liked or accepted	Losing control
Accounting for money spent	Being overlooked at promotion
Living by the clock or someone	time
keeping score	Not being able to produce
	(through illness or redundancy)

PEACEFUL	PRECISE
Being the one made	Not being understood
accountable	Having to compromise standards
Major changes	Making too many mistakes
The buck stopping with them	
(they prefer it to be shared)	
Confrontation	

ANSWERS AND REPONSES TO EXPECT

PLAYFUL	POWERFUL
Personal	Short and precise
Creative	Pointed and direct
Ego-driven	

PEACEFUL	PRECISE
Qualified statements	Qualified
Tactful	Technical
Hesitant to give an opinion	Unimaginative
	Precise
	Following policy and rules

CLOTHING

PLAYFUL	POWERFUL
Stylish	Functional and practical
Flamboyant	Dress how they want to
Eye-catching	Appearance is likely to impress (in a powerful way!)
Latest fashion, making them noticeable to others	Spend little attention on this issue unless it is vital to outcomes

PEACEFUL	PRECISE
Conservative and casual	Classic
Conventional styles	Well-groomed
Trainers a must	Quiet
Comfortable	Hair always in place (except for hippie types)
Subtle, calming colours	Unobtrusive, but quality
	Impeccably dressed
	Tastes may be somewhat different from others'
	Dark colours e.g. khaki, black, grey

PLAYFUL	POWERFUL
Limit what you say, conveying only what is vital	Request (not demand!) others' action
Halve your stories	Say 'please' and 'thank you' more often
Listen — and try not to interrupt	Be careful of tone of voice
Try to remember people's names	Stay in one place (do not pace around or leave the room)
If interrupted, continue only if asked	Focus interest and relevance on the person, not the project
Tone down	Actively listen — don't cut others off
Seek others' comments	Try not to talk over people and finish other people's sentences or stories
Be inclusive of those not speaking	Respect others by reading all their contributions

PEACEFUL	PRECISE
Express your opinion — you have something to say	Watch for opportunities to encourage others
More volume	Give incremental compliments
Move more quickly	Bestow praise instead of criticism
Plan and think through what has to be done in advance	Realise there is no perfection
Stay engaged	Focus on good character traits
Share ideas	Give less information
Show enthusiasm through expression, level of interest and body language	Receive compliments graciously
	Practise making positive observations
	Show non-verbal acceptance

COMMUNICATING WITH A . . .

PLAYFUL	POWERFUL
Tell stories about your life	Speak in condensed form
Give lots of exciting information	Give them appreciation for all their achievements
Show acceptance	Include results and bottom line information
Pay attention	Support with detail only if asked, or if you have been attacked verbally by them
Show approval	Accept abruptness — they are not intentionally rude but can come across that way
Stay tuned	Be project focused

PEACEFUL	PRECISE
Show respect	Be polite
Look for positives	Don't interrupt them if they are busy
Give only a few choices — make it easy for them	Respect their time, space, silence and schedule
Give praise freely	Don't pry and delve into their personal life
Learn to say 'I appreciate your [attribute]' rather than what they have done	Give factual, orderly details
Give concentrated attention	Laugh and cry with them, but don't try to jolly them up when blue
Wait to respond until they are completely finished	Prepare — think through what you are going to say

COMMUNICATION STYLE

PLAYFUL	POWERFUL
Open	In your face
Expressive body language	Can be intimidating with gestures
Loves to connect by touch	Gives quick commands or orders
An incessant talker, regardless if anyone is listening	Doesn't tolerate chit-chat
Loud	Cuts off others mid-sentence and finishes others' stories
Belly laugh	Says 'Cut to the chase!', 'Get to the point!'
Speaks first, then thinks	
Will talk to anyone, anywhere, anytime	Single-minded, task-oriented
Tell stories about life's little disasters	Restless, moving on once they have grasped the concept
People-oriented	Can dismiss others

PEACEFUL	PRECISE
Relaxed, open body language	'The Thinker'
Calming presence where others are stressed out	Gestures close to body
	Precise and accurate
Speaks only when they have something of value to say	Speaks when they feel they can contribute
Hesitant to offer opinions	Not keen to open up about their life
Uninvolved	Shares only with those close
Soft voice	Thinks, then speaks
Dry humour	Shares only on a need-to-know basis
Good listener	Prefers the written word
Accommodating	Justice and fairness imperative
People-oriented	Task-oriented

CONTROL BY . . .

PLAYFUL	POWERFUL
Luring and captivating	Threat of an outburst and tension
Charming	'Remember what happened last
'Oh honey, you'll do that so well	time you did that?'
Come on, give it a go!'	

PEACEFUL	PRECISE
Purposely delaying and putting off	Threat of displeasure
'Why do today what you can put	Throws everyone into a guessing
off for tomorrow?'	game
	'Something wrong?' 'No, nothing . . .'

CONVERSATIONS AROUND . . .

PLAYFUL	POWERFUL
People and relationships	Organisation
Life's little disasters and tragedies,	Results
made light of	Outcomes and bottom lines
Emotional intelligence	Efficiency and growth
Decisions made from their feelings	Things they want to accomplish
	(They don't care if you don't
	like them)

PEACEFUL	PRECISE
Security	Facts/logic
Risks one can avoid	History
Systems	Decisions made from an
Hobbies	intellectual basis
Finding easy ways to do things	How to do specific things

DECISION-MAKING

PLAYFUL	POWERFUL
Impulsive	Decisive
Erratic	Quick
On basis of personal motivation	Calculated risks
Big picture	
Status quo	

PEACEFUL	PRECISE
Slow, sure and studied	Objective
Avoids being different, so will often make decisions on that basis	Cautious
	Decides only after getting all the facts and processing them in a logical way
May not decide until they know what others think and feel	
Avoids risks	

DEMOTIVATORS — THINGS THAT DISCOURAGE

PLAYFUL	POWERFUL
When there is no fun and work is boring	When they can't be in control

PEACEFUL	PRECISE
Too many changes and being pushed too hard	Too many mistakes being made
Conflict	

DEPRESSION — CAN BE TRIGGERED BY . . .

PLAYFUL	POWERFUL
Feeling as if life is no fun Feeling alienated	Feeling as if life is out of their control and they can't do a thing about it

PEACEFUL	PRECISE
Having far too many problems to deal with	Disappointments Feeling overwhelmed Little hope of change

EMAILS

PLAYFUL	POWERFUL
Always begins with a personal story or question Gets caught up in the dialogue, then forgets the reason they needed to write Usually includes a joke or funny story Lots of !!!!!! and :-)	Bullet or action points Can overlook saying 'please' and 'thank you' by focusing on the big picture Straight up and to the point

PEACEFUL	PRECISE
Remembers names of client's family Starts on a relationship level, then addresses the issue Never demanding or straight up Never pushy	Writes the longest emails, containing all the data required Ticks off all action points Well written — no mistakes More formal than other personalities

ENVIRONMENT

PLAYFUL	POWERFUL
Lots of clutter and mess	Awards and signs of recognition

PEACEFUL	PRECISE
Old relics and mementoes	Charts and graphs
	Academic achievements

FEAR — HOW THEY EXPRESS IT

PLAYFUL	POWERFUL
Loud	Sucks it in
Expresses fear openly	Very rarely shows fear
Squeals and is dramatic	

PEACEFUL	PRECISE
Physical display of trembling	Internalises fear
Beads of sweat	Talks their way through it
Fear hidden	

FOCUS ON . . .

PLAYFUL	POWERFUL
People	The job
Process and people	Results and bottom line

PEACEFUL	PRECISE
The way things need to be done	The best possible way to do it
Process and systems	Results and structure

GESTURES

PLAYFUL	POWERFUL
Largest of all gestures	Fast
Inviting	Direct
	Restless

PEACEFUL	PRECISE
Measured	Closed
Relaxed	Private
Gentle	Formal
Fluid	Proper

GETTING ALONG WITH A . . .

PLAYFUL	POWERFUL
Try to help them not accept everything they volunteer for	Realise they are movers and doers
Realise they like lots of variation and flexibility to their day	Be aware they are the born leaders
Understand they have to work at time management	Be gutsy, and insist there is a two-way conversation
Encourage them when they accomplish something	Know they don't mean to hurt, they are just upfront
Remember they are circumstantial people	Realise it's not natural for them to feel compassionate
They love surprises, gifts and fun encounters	They don't suffer fools

PEACEFUL	PRECISE
Realise they need direct motivation	Because they are very sensitive, they can get hurt easily
Help them set goals and give them incremental rewards	Remember they are naturally wired with a cautious attitude
Don't expect enthusiasm — it doesn't come easy	Learn about depression and how it impacts on them
Lovingly help them to make decisions	Show loving and sincere support
Champion them to accept responsibilities	Appreciate that for them, peace and quiet are up there with oxygen
Don't dump on them	Don't be late — they value good time-keeping
Wait until they speak	Give ideas with supporting data
	They don't like surprises

GREAT FOR . . .

PLAYFUL	POWERFUL
Bringing fun back into the equation	Clear thinking
Simplicity	Keeping control when others are losing it
Re-starting things	Leadership
Ideas and creativity	Opposing others or standing alone
	Seeing the big picture

PEACEFUL	PRECISE
Keeping on course	Being artistic, creative
Putting up with troublemakers	Having an eye for detail
Listening while others speak	Doing things well
Patience	Completing tasks
Uniting opposing teams	Making something out of nothing
Mediation	Strategic planning
Finishing the hard jobs other people avoid	Procedures

HOW THEY WORK

PLAYFUL	POWERFUL
Quickly	Hard
Can go off on tangents	Prefer to work on their own

PEACEFUL	PRECISE
Constant, steady and reliable	Accurate/Deliberate
Great at finishing tasks	Diligent and responsible

IDENTIFYING PERSONALITIES THROUGH THEIR ACTIONS

PLAYFUL	POWERFUL
Spontaneous; Friendly; Animated; Loud; Confident; Entertaining; Big ego; Enjoys social and business recognition; Elegant; Lives up to income; Dislikes writing reports; Disorganised; Verbal rather than written communication	Thrives on challenges; Task- rather than people-oriented; Powerful and prestigious; Restless; Impatient; Decisive; Impulsive; Quick; Change agent; Direct; Abrupt; Can argue one minute and laugh the next; Big ego; May lack empathy; Likes to juggle many tasks or interests at one time

PEACEFUL	PRECISE
Mature; Sincere; Warm; Good listener; Friendly manner; Steady but high performer; Great team player; Gives loyalty and expects it in return; Feels deeply, but usually holds in emotions; Modest; Unassuming; Patient; Dependable; Responsible; Seemingly easy going, but can be stubborn; Cares deeply about family and colleagues	Problem-solver; Critical; Prepares and plans well; Perfectionist; Quality controllor; Mind like a steel trap; Worries, particularly about solutions; Sensitive to criticism Abhors making errors; Follows directions precisely;Analyser; Thinker; Intuitive; Likes facts and logic; Accurate; Dislikes carelessness or disorder; Does not like overly aggressive people; Neat and organised dress, desk, home and car

IF THIS PERSONALITY WAS A COUNTRY . . .

PLAYFUL	POWERFUL
Spain — lots of expression	Japan — short and to the point

PEACEFUL	PRECISE
Switzerland — prefers to listen and keep the peace	England — speaks The Queen's English, well thought-out

KEY PHRASE

PLAYFUL	POWERFUL
'Look at me!'	'Appreciate me'

PEACEFUL	PRECISE
'Respect me'	'Understand me'

LEADERSHIP STYLE

PLAYFUL	POWERFUL
Inspirational	Visionary
Charismatic	Big picture
Charming	Naturally in charge
Optimistic	Quick insight into what will work
Fun	Self-belief in their ability to achieve
Motivational	Upfront and candid

PEACEFUL	PRECISE
Diplomatic	Strategic
Strong mediator	Critical thinker
Cool, calm and collected	Organises well
Not impulsive in decision-making	Sensitive to people's needs
Well-liked	Artistically creative
Inoffensive	Wants quality performance
Nurturer	Project driven

LIKES TO TALK ABOUT . . .

PLAYFUL	POWERFUL
Interaction with others	Competence and business
(People)	(Tasks)

PEACEFUL	PRECISE
Safety measures	Specifics and reasoning
The tried and true	(Tasks)
(People and Process)	

LISTENING SKILLS

PLAYFUL	POWERFUL
Drifts in and out of conversations	Impatient and restless

PEACEFUL	PRECISE
Willing and brilliant	Selective

MANNER

PLAYFUL	POWERFUL
Pleasant and friendly	'Doer' Strong presence Dominating

PEACEFUL	PRECISE
Accepting and affable	Assessing and evaluating

MEETINGS

PLAYFUL	POWERFUL
Interrupts, goes off on tangents Distracted	Dominates

PEACEFUL	PRECISE
Prefers to listen Favourite word 'Whatever'	Strong critical skills

MOTIVATION

PLAYFUL	POWERFUL
Recognition	Recognition

PEACEFUL	PRECISE
Security	Security

NEEDS

PLAYFUL	POWERFUL
Attention	Credit for their abilities and
Affection	accomplishments
Approval	To achieve
Acceptance	Loyalty

PEACEFUL	PRECISE
To feel valued	Sensitivity
Respect and a feeling of	Space
worth	Silence
Peace and quiet	Support

NEEDS TO DO MORE . . .

PLAYFUL	POWERFUL
Active listening	Saying 'please' and 'thank you'
	Listening

PEACEFUL	PRECISE
Speaking up	Making positive observations

NEEDS TO KNOW . . .

PLAYFUL	POWERFUL
Who?	What/when?
Emphasis on people	Emphasis on results

PEACEFUL	PRECISE
Why?	How?
Emphasis on reason why	Emphasis on details

PACE

PLAYFUL	POWERFUL
Enthusiastic	Fast

PEACEFUL	PRECISE
Steady	Controlled

PROUD OF . . .

PLAYFUL	POWERFUL
Relationships	Achievements
Creativity	Working hard

PEACEFUL	PRECISE
Relationships and friends	Using process to reach a logical
Keeping the peace	conclusion
	Detail and order

QUESTIONS THEY WILL ASK

PLAYFUL	POWERFUL
Personal	Short
Creative	Precise
	Objective-driven

PEACEFUL	PRECISE
Around process and people	Logical and fact-oriented
How things can be done	For support
	About process
	Asking for technical details

RECOVERS BY . . .

PLAYFUL	POWERFUL
Partying with fun people	Physical activity — running, working out, physical work

PEACEFUL	PRECISE
'Nothing' time — just sitting down doing nothing	Quiet time — going off by themselves

RELATIONSHIPS

PLAYFUL	POWERFUL
Identifies with others	Commands others

PEACEFUL	PRECISE
Accepting of others	Assesses others

RESPONSIVENESS

PLAYFUL	POWERFUL
Friendly	Impatient
Obliging	Restless

PEACEFUL	PRECISE
Steady	Cool
Reserved	Distant

SENSE OF HUMOUR

PLAYFUL	POWERFUL
'Let me tell you what happened the other day . . . '	'Just kidding — really!'
Storyteller	Joke-teller
Situational humour	Variety of types of humour, that can be delivered quickly and have a point
Ribs others	Smiler
Variety of types of humour that allow exaggeration	
Hearty belly laughter	

PEACEFUL	PRECISE
'Now that's funny!'	'Humph!'
Quick, original wit	Sense of humour is their best-kept secret!
Uses one-liners, absurdity, puns, irony	Rarely delivers humour except with close friends and family
Excellent ability to use humour to defuse tense situations	Internalises humour
Can be tinged with sarcasm	Values all humour, but especially analytical, thinking humour
Chuckler	Stoic expression

SHOPPING STYLE

PLAYFUL	POWERFUL
Impulsive, fun-loving buyer	Practical, decisive buyer
Shops anytime	Focused shopper
Spendthrift	Decides ahead of time what they
Loves shopping — enjoys crowds	want
Easily swayed	Controls shopping time
Tries the latest things	Avoids crowds
Enjoys an expedition with others	Judicious about trying new things
Never has enough money!	Savvy about money
Charms salesperson	Intimidates salesperson

PEACEFUL	PRECISE
Uninvolved, relaxed buyer	State-of-the-art, bottom-line buyer
Delays shopping time	Schedules shopping time
Frugal in their spending	Budget-oriented
Loves a bargain	Seeks bargains
Avoids crowds	Makes lists of stores and cross-
Prefers small stores and makes	references items
repeat visits	Battles crowds alone
Wants few choices	Needs time to evaluate
Needs encouragement	Cautious about new things
Procrastinating buyer	Critical, nit-picking
Not free with their money	Frugal with money
Puzzles salesperson	Ignores salesperson

SMALL TALK

PLAYFUL	POWERFUL
Loves small talk	Minimal to none
Personal interest	Industry inclination
Positive	

PEACEFUL	PRECISE
Comfortable with small talk	Some small talk
	Technical in nature
	Project-oriented
	Around tasks
	Nothing personal

SPEECH

PLAYFUL	POWERFUL
Enthusiastic	Friendly, but may be abrupt
Expressive	Little emotion
Lots of variety in pitch	Authoritative
Laughs loud and a lot	Rapid pace
	Gives the Readers' Digest condensed version

PEACEFUL	PRECISE
Friendly	Facts and logic
Excellent listener	Cautious and non-committal
May have monotonous voice	Reserved
Slow pace, with warmth	Slow pace
Measured	Limited emotion
	Closed
	Cool, calm and collected

STRENGTHS

PLAYFUL	POWERFUL
Fun; Adventurous; Initiator; Creative and visual thinker; Can function in chaos; Lives in the present; Loves variety, flexibility, change; Spontaneous/boisterous; Most forgiving of all types	Able to take charge of anything; Has a need for excitement; Fast-moving approach; Can make quick, correct judgements; Great decision-maker; Restless; Confident; Single-minded; Doer, not a watcher; Good under pressure
PEACEFUL	**PRECISE**
Steady; Balanced; Dependable; No extremes; Calm; Patient; Wonderful listener; Compassionate; Can work under pressure; Keeps people happy and produces few enemies; Loyal; Dedicated; Co-operative; Pleasant; Believable; Retentive mind; Brings order out of chaos; Delegates well; Great Integrity; Steady performer and team player	Thoughtful; Well-mannered; Meticulous ; Well-groomed; Conservative; Energised by their 'inner world'; Focused; Organised; Gets more enjoyment from music and fine arts; Eye for detail; Economical; Persistent; Mind like a steel trap; Loves analysis; Likes to make careful decisions

STRESS RELIEF

PLAYFUL	POWERFUL
Moments of fun	Separation from out-of-control or
Freedom from restrictions and	uncontrollable situations
schedules	Physical activity
	Starting a new project

PEACEFUL	PRECISE
Time alone	Personal space
'Nothing' time	Meticulousness
Turning on the TV and escaping	Long stretches of silence and space

STRESS RESPONSES

PLAYFUL	POWERFUL
Overspending	Outbursts
Blaming others	Physical exertion
Finding a fun group	Getting rid of the offender

PEACEFUL	PRECISE
Hiding from it	Recounting the problems
Watching TV	Whining
Eating	Negative thinking
Fading to back	

TEAM CONTRIBUTION

PLAYFUL	POWERFUL
Innovation, ideas and creativity	Declaration and focus

PEACEFUL	PRECISE
Diplomacy and nurturing	Organisation and quality control

TELEPHONE MANNER

PLAYFUL	POWERFUL
Expressive	Friendly, but may be abrupt
Laughter and kidding	Authoritative and direct
Welcoming	Fast pace, with little emotion
Plenty of variation in voice tone	
Fast pace, with lots of emotion	

PEACEFUL	PRECISE
Friendly	May not commit to requests
Brilliant listener	immediately
May be hesitant to respond	Asks a lot of questions
Slow pace, with warmth and	Abhors pushy callers
friendliness	Slow pace, with limited emotion
	and enthusiasm

TIME — ATTITUDE TO

PLAYFUL	POWERFUL
Socialises at the cost of time	Time is of the essence

PEACEFUL	PRECISE
Respects time, but rarely pushed	Values and manages time well

TIME-MANAGEMENT CHALLENGES

PLAYFUL	POWERFUL
Over-commits	Under-plans
Tendency to be late	Not detail oriented
Unorganised by nature	Killer 'to do' lists
Forgetful	No time for rest and relaxation
Solution: be brief	Solution: get to the bottom line

PEACEFUL	PRECISE
Under-commits	Over-plans
Procrastinates	Perfectionism leads to
Lack of energy	procrastination
Not goal-oriented	Cannot function in chaos
Solution: be patient	Solution: be deliberate

TRUST BUILT BY . . .

PLAYFUL	POWERFUL
Openness	Conformity

PEACEFUL	PRECISE
Harmony	Acquiescence

TRUST SABOTAGED BY . . .

PLAYFUL	POWERFUL
Not being listened to	Judgement or 'murmurings' in the
Non-approval	ranks

PEACEFUL	PRECISE
Disagreement	Being closed

TYPE OF PERSON

PLAYFUL	POWERFUL
Impetuous	Resolute

PEACEFUL	PRECISE
Nonchalant	Guarded

UNDER PRESSURE

PLAYFUL	POWERFUL
Throws a hissy fit	Becomes an oppressor

PEACEFUL	PRECISE
Pretends to conform	Withdraws and internalises

VOCATION

PLAYFUL	POWERFUL
Any place there are people	Any place they can control and have influence

PEACEFUL	PRECISE
Conciliation	Detail and order
Systematic and repetitive jobs	Difficult roles

WEAKNESSES

PLAYFUL	POWERFUL
Haphazard	Impatient
Talking too much	Domineering
Loud	Terse
Disorganised	Bullying
Messy	Imposing
Forgetful	

PEACEFUL	PRECISE
Intractable	Critical
Indecisive	Pedantic
Slow	Whiny
Selfish	Unforgiving

WHAT OTHER PERSONALITIES NEED

PLAYFUL	POWERFUL
Give them an ear	Keep conversation short and to the point
Show approval through your body language — nodding, smiling, eye contact etc.	Appreciate all they have achieved
Bring energy to the conversation	Always communicate the bottom line and results
Affirm them	Only give details if asked
Include stories, particularly about life's little disasters	Accept that they can come across terse and curt. They don't mean to be rude, they're just focused
Use analogies and metaphors	Keep conversation moving
Engage their imagination	Give credit
Use very little detail	

PEACEFUL	PRECISE
Focus on the process	Use manners and courtesies
Show respect and value them for their caring, calming influence	Don't interrupt them
Give praise liberally	Give them time, space, silence and support
Stay in the moment	Don't probe their privacy
Listen and don't butt in	Think before you speak, and make it clear and concise
Give them few choices	Give details not chit-chat
Don't expect many questions or immediate decisions	Appeal to their sense of fairness
Talk about the tried and true, guarantees and security	Always be on time
They don't like latest fads	Stick with the plans made
Talk about people concerns	
Be friendly and considerate	

WHEN OTHERS ANNOY US, WE SEE THEM AS . . .

PLAYFUL	POWERFUL
Artificial	Thick-skinned
Fickle	Arrogant

PEACEFUL	PRECISE
Weak-willed	Picky
Wavering	Lacklustre

WORK BEST IN THIS ENVIRONMENT . . .

PLAYFUL	POWERFUL
People and fun	Command and influence

PEACEFUL	PRECISE
Mediation and repetition	Quiet
Free from conflict	Detail and structure

WORKING STYLE

PLAYFUL	POWERFUL
Quick	Hard
Thrives around people	

PEACEFUL	PRECISE
Constant	Accurate
No stress	Likes to work alone

WORK STRENGTHS

PLAYFUL	POWERFUL
Creative	Focused
New ideas	Big picture
Extremes	Action-oriented
Starts with full gusto	Productive
Inclusive	Goal-oriented
Energy and fervour	Keeps things moving
Inspires others	Practical and logical
	Doesn't mind the threat of opposition

PEACEFUL	PRECISE
Steady	Orderly and detailed
Dependable	Cost-conscious
Reliable	Reliable
Works well under pressure	Loves problem-solving
Looks for short cuts	Creative in finding solutions
Dodges conflict	Time-keeper
Brilliant administrator	Stickler
Mediates problems	Stayer
Good finisher	Good finisher
	Thrives on lists
	Loves difficult problems

WORK WEAKNESSES

PLAYFUL	POWERFUL
Starts well, but quickly fades and loses interest	Demanding and controlling of others
Finds the hard yards difficult	Little tolerance for trivia
Difficult to keep on track	Doesn't care how it gets done (end justifies the means)
Talking rather than action	Mistakes not tolerated
Wrong priorities	Delegates only when they can get a piece of the praise
Goes by feelings	Doesn't analyse details
Easily sidetracked	Quick and rash decisions
Wastes time talking	Can come across terse and rude
Gets bored quickly	Manipulates people

PEACEFUL	PRECISE
Not goal oriented	Would rather work alone
Needs others to motivate them	Frustrated by mistakes
Digs their toes in when pushed	Spends too much time planning and preparing
Would rather share the job	High ideals mean very little encouragement comes from them because it's never good enough
Doesn't like initiating	
Can discourage others who have lots of ideas	Can't stand noise
Doesn't volunteer much	Never forgets a slight — real or imagined

Further reading

Allison Mooney *Read my LIPS*, self-published (Australia, PO Box 1171, Mooloolaba, Queensland 4557, Australia)

Allison Mooney *How to navigate through a marketing minefield*, self-published (Australia, PO Box 1171, Mooloolaba, Queensland 4557, Australia)

Florence Littauer (1983 and 1992) *Personality Plus*, Fleming H Revell

Florence Littauer (1986) *Your Personality Tree*, W Publishing Group

Florence Littauer (2000) *Personality Plus for Couples*, Fleming H Revell

Florence Littauer (2000) *Personality Plus for Parents*, Fleming H Revell

Marita Littauer with insights from Florence Littauer (2006) *Wired that Way*, Regal Books

www.personalities.co.nz

Acknowledgements

When I first came to an understanding of personalities, my main passion and drive was to get this message out. I'd talk to anyone who wanted to listen. In fact I became a bit of an evangelist about it. It was hard not — it had helped me so much, I wanted to share it with as many people possible. As I have been on the speaking circuit now for over a decade, I saw the next sensible phase was to write, - a natural progression in my development. I knew also I would get the message out to places I never thought possible.

Now let's see who has been **pressing the right buttons** for me.

I can't proceed any further without acknowledging Florence and the late Fred Littauer for all the teaching and extreme generosity they have showered on me regarding the subject of understanding people. The first night I heard Florence, I purchased 11 of her books. I was so ready. The desire for food came nowhere near the appetite I had for this new-found knowledge. Florence's ability to share stories in the most metaphorical and impacting way certainly made a lot of sense to me. Not only that, but these principles truly work when applied. I would not be where I am today without this inspirational and worthy role model. Their daughter Marita is worthy of acknowledgement and has picked up the vision for this work — thank you for your continued support.

I feel most humble, and acknowledge today the privilege of not only carrying a message, but of being able to deliver and share it, particularly in the business sector.

The hot issues in the business marketplace today are staff retention, skill shortage, a tight labour market, and employment tribunal problems. These are impacting enormously on the bottom line, a huge concern for business owners. Feedback I get from leaders tells me that one of the main reasons why people get restless and want to leave their jobs, is because of difficulties they have with fellow colleagues. Personality clashes we call them. There is also an inability to motivate, move and inspire people. Perhaps they need to understand that we all need motivating in different ways. The incredible investment that goes in to training a new recruit, only to have them leave because of their frustration at being undervalued, costs organisations millions of dollars every year, when applying a few 'people skills' would have kept them there.

I want to say 'thank you' to those organisations that see the value in investing in their people this way. Too many to name, but you are part of the success of this message as you have benefited by advancing your people through this simple but powerful tool.

For me this understanding has so enhanced my marriage, and helped me get even closer to my children.

Now for me to do what I am doing, I can't tell you how much I have looked forward to the opportunity to acknowledge and thank my family. My gorgeous husband Brian who has done a brilliant job at keeping the home fires burning, and the tax man from the door (keeping my GST and tax in order) while I have written. After a day's work you have come home and sometimes had to eat Baked Beans because I was in my office furiously trying to get this finished. All those extra jobs you took on, and the many tasks around the house that it hasn't been possible for me to complete. Never once did I hear you complain. You have always encouraged me in my strengths, and believed the best of me. You have been willing to do those mundane tasks that keep my business and home ticking over, even learning to cook. This experience has proved we have become great partners in our marriage and business. This book is completed because of your patience, love and confidence in me.

My darling daughters. Always checking to see if I am OK. Brilliant at protecting me from myself. I do have a weak spot: over-commitment. They have had to be bull terriers at times, but only because they want to see me live a long time, for which I am so grateful. Thank you Shay and Kyleigh, you mean the world to me.

My grandson Josh (who energises me). I love hanging out with him. I love watching him teach me things. Josh you are described in this book, and I hope you will understand it all and run with your incredible gifts and talents as you grow. Bob, my new son-in-law who looks after my daughter so well. I am developing a relational book, and you will certainly be in this. You are so easy to identify.

To Zena my sister, who continues to inspire me by going back to university at 60 to get her degree. I kept that foremost in my mind as I wrote. If she can do that, well, I can write a book! A formidable woman.

I couldn't forget two wonderful 'full of life' extraordinary women, Fleur Whelligan and Kim Morrison who opened the door for me to write this book. They are a few up on me — but who is counting? When I attended one of their book launches, I heard from them, that writing a book was like giving birth. I am glad I didn't hear that before I started. Anyone who is a speaker first and then a writer will agree. Those who are writers first may not agree. I am a speaker first, then a writer. The goal to get this message to the business world has held me captive for these nine long months and has been my driving force. I have been very sick, but the flame didn't die even then. Thank you, you two phenomenal women. You both have a place in my heart. Thank you for stretching me and spurring me on.

To my close girlfriends who gave up their social coffees and heart to hearts with me, so I could stay focused and write this book. How I have missed you all. I hope we have enough in our emotional bank account that I can call you soon for a catch up. I could never have done this without your presence in my life.

To all those who championed me, especially those wonderful business associates who gave me great stories to put into this book. Too many to name, but one is James Hamilton, who gave me one of my first paid public speaking jobs, and has walked the journey alongside me and given me feedback and encouragement now for many years. I want to acknowledge Michelle Henderson, Annette Williams, Val McGregor, Katrina Winn, Jennie Farrar deWagt, Christine McGrail and Rebecca Mathews. I want to particularly mention The National Speakers Association of New Zealand, an outstanding organisation. I have never been in a more encouraging industry that spurs you on. For those I haven't mentioned by name but you know who you are — I appreciate you so much. You are part of this success.

To Random House for their guidance, encouragement and experience in this new frontier for me, you have done a splendid job.

Last but certainly not least, to my nephew Leon. Yes, you are one remarkable and genuine man. You have taught me so much about grace, leadership and living life in the moment. You are such an inspiration to me and I dedicate this book to you because, against all odds, with a disease that has robbed you of truly breaking out in your body, you have stunned everyone and shown the medical authorities that no one can deliver a sentence on anyone else's life. You remain free of prejudices, free of intellectual limitations, and have kept a gentle and beautiful spirit through it all. That is why you are so appealing and attractive to those who walk into your room. Every day you choose to have a remarkable attitude to life. That puts you up there with the 'greats' of this world. How rich I am having you in my life. You are my inspiration.

Index